DARE TO BE
DIFFERENT

AN AUDITORS PERSONAL GUIDE
TO EXCELLENCE

DANIEL CLARK

Order this book online at www.trafford.com
or email orders@trafford.com

Most Trafford titles are also available at major online book retailers.

Print information available on the last page.

ISBN: 978-1-4907-7240-0 (sc)
ISBN: 978-1-4907-7238-7 (hc)
ISBN: 978-1-4907-7239-4 (e)

Library of Congress Control Number: 2016906348

Trafford rev.   04/22/2016

 www.trafford.com

North America & international
toll-free: 1 888 232 4444 (USA & Canada)
fax: 812 355 4082

Contents

Enderosements

Worked for Dan at GE Capital for two years. Let me sum it up . . . he has forgotten more about auditing than most people will ever know! Excellent manager and very articulate in communications. Well regarded in the company.

—Michael Marcucci CRC, CIA—Risk and Audit Executive

As an audit leader, Dan has instilled in his teams the need to look beyond the obvious, searching for anomalies in data, overly complicated processes and anything that doesn't seem right. By applying a common sense approach, his teams are able to identify true risks and sound recommendations for remediation. By keeping things "light," he's effective at obtaining buy-in for his suggestions.

—Olivia Gallegos Independent Consultant and former CAE Global Consumer Banking

Auditing may be a dry area for many professionals, but definitely becomes a very rich and rewarding topic when you have a leader that challenges you and guides you at identifying the real risks and issues of the institution. Dan was for me that leader and continues to be a mentor to whom I reach when I need independent fair feedback on significant decisions in my career. As a risk professional, I appreciate the audit analytical skills and creativity that I learned from Dan as those have complemented the acumen that today I share with my clients.

—Elizabeth Marvan, Executive Director Rhisco

Dan is a progressive audit executive. He challenges the status quo and constantly pushes audit teams to raise the bar. When Dan came on board at GE Capital, I found him to be a quick learner, and a valued colleague and partner. Over the years we worked together, I was impressed with his financial and operational expertise, his tactful management of challenging situations (and stakeholders), and his ever-present optimism.

—Cathy Miron, Strategic Initiatives Leader, Cloud at GE

Preface

During the many years that I have had the pleasure of working as an auditor, I have noticed that our profession has seen nonstop change and evolution. Our industry watchdogs have applauded us and, in some instances, been a little less generous in their opinions of our work. The regulators, the professional associations, and our clients have changed. All are evolving, either emerging or regressing, depending on the situation, topic, or organization. Through it all we, the auditors, have remained steadfast in our efforts to perform to standard and contribute value to the organizations we serve.

I have to be honest. I am not your typical auditor. While I do have an audit certification, I am not a CPA, nor do I sit on any industry board or leadership committee. My background is successful business experience and risk management. I came to the profession quite by accident joining a rotational program at a large international bank. I was supposed to stay for three years and go back to the business. After more than eighteen years, I am still in audit. I have to confess that I am not sure whether that is because no one in the business wanted me anymore or just because I really found the transformation that audit was experiencing and will continue to experience fascinating. I will assume it is the latter because who in the business would not want me to work for them?

Through it all I have learned a few things. Not because I am smarter than anyone else but just because I learned them. This book is all about those observations and lessons learned. After eighteen years as an audit leader, three times as chief auditor, something had to stick. What that something was is an understanding of what it takes to become an excellent auditor. Not from a one dimensional technical perspective, as most people would expect, but from the multifaceted personal perspective. It is that perspective that can transform an auditor and help them achieve their best potential. More importantly, it will add value to your work.

This book is not about technical training. It is not about presentations, issue writing, or use of analytics. It is also not about just being successful. Unlike any other book available to our industry, this book solely focuses on what it takes for you, the individual, to excel at our profession. By using real life examples and *Keys to Excellence*, once read, and continued to be referred to, this book will ensure that you excel as an auditor. I encourage you to "Dare to be Different!"

Secrets to Defining "You"

Unlike conventional wisdom which states that it is all about the client, the customer, the spouse, or the child, it really is all about you. People may argue and say that I am a bit self-centered. But let them scream. If it was about them they would probably be heard. But it's not about them it is all about me, or better stated, it is all about "you." However, before we get too carried away, let me preface that statement by defining what "all about *you*" really implies.

Auditing is a profession that is not done in isolation. The days of one person audits should be over. Even with the advances in technology and the massive abilities to provide remote audit techniques and tools, auditing in isolation is not the answer. So if you are thinking that "it" being all about "you" is focused only on you, you are sorely mistaken. The "you" we are referring to here is your brand: that "something" that defines you: that "something" that separates you from the rest of the crowd. That "something" that tells people what you are all about. It is that "something" that permits people to recognize how you fit into the team and how you make the team better.

Constructing a personal brand is tricky and warrants significant thought and planning. There are several books about brand management or personal branding circulating in the market place today. It would be worthwhile to review some of those as you create and define your personal brand. That being said, no matter what your brand looks like or how well you define it, there are seven key characteristics that you must demonstrate if you are to excel at your profession.

Insight and Foresight

While working for a large international banking organization, I had a number of bosses. Some were quite good, some were okay and some, well let's say, should have read my book. One of my favorite instances occurred when one of those bosses asked me what auditors get paid for providing. I was hoping that this would lead up to my annual review and salary increase so I responded with things like quality products, well-written reports, meaningful issues, etc., etc., etc. I was wrong. The conversation did not lead up to my salary review.

"Auditors get paid for their insight," he said.

"Face it, Dan, anyone can be an auditor. Companies hire people fresh out of college and poof, they are auditors. We bring people in from the line of business and "poof," they are auditors. We can find an auditor almost anywhere we look and they all do the same thing. They gather data, perform tests, they find exceptions, report the exceptions, and move on to the next assignment. A great business telling people what they probably already know.

"The best auditor though has learned that the personal differentiator in this profession is the insight one provides his client," he continued.

I have given his message much thought and I believe it as it has been proven to me time and time again.

There are two definitions for "Insight" that appropriately relate to our profession:

> —an instance of apprehending the true nature of a thing, especially through intuitive understanding
> —penetrating mental vision or discernment; faculty of seeing into inner character or underlying truth

If we explore these a little deeper, there are two aspects of the definitions that the best auditor will leverage: (1) intuitive understanding, and (2) discernment.

In one of the companies I have had the opportunity to work for, I was surrounded by brilliant fast-trackers. These individuals were selected to participate in a leadership process that was demanding but would lead to great career rewards. The leadership program's basic premise was to use an audit-like process to train these future leaders. I have to admit, I have seldom seen a group of individuals so dedicated, so smart, so willing to put in all required time to excel at what they did. To this day, it still has to be one of the most successful audit organizations in the world. But is it the best? Not at all!

The biggest downfall, one that even they don't recognize, is that they do not have the intuitive understanding required to be the best auditors. While educational pedigrees were remarkable, the practical business experience required to gain intuitive understanding did not yet exist. And unfortunately, for all their smarts, they often failed to listen to those who did have that experience.

I am not saying that only auditors who worked as business leaders can be the best because that would be untrue. In fact, there are many challenges faced by business leaders converting to the audit profession. But having experience, or funneling the experience of business line management into your thought processes, certainly puts you one leg up on everyone else.

Moving from insight to foresight is the mark that sets you apart from every other auditor. While so many of our industry struggle with providing insight, there is plenty of room for those who can learn to predict future events and their impact and communicate that well. I don't mean that we use models to predict portfolio losses, or test assumptions to determine if weightings are correct. I am talking about the ability to use all the knowledge we have gained and be able to construct a legitimate argument based on intuitive abilities (matching experience with insight) that helps our client tomorrow.

So here is the first *Key to Excellence.*

Build expertise through personal experience or the experience of others so that your intuitive abilities grow.

If you don't have the direct experience, you may want to consider this tidbit from Henry Ford. Once asked if he knew the details about certain aspects of his business he responded, "No, but I know who to talk with to find out." So if you want to be the best, build an inner network of experts that will be honest and candid with you and use them to gain insights that you may not have.

The second Key to Excellence is:

Master the art of discernment. Things are usually exactly what they are not what people want you to believe they are!

The Japanese have a wonderful approach to life. Among many aspects of their beautiful culture, one stands out to me. They believe that things are simply what they are. Today we say "it is what it is" and that has become a catch phrase for explaining things away. For westerners, and especially for business leaders, it is more an excuse than a way of life. Not for the Japanese. They have the ability to discern exactly what something is, the role that something has, and <u>not to give undue importance to anything</u>.

Have you ever noticed how the first issues you discover as an auditor are really important? I have always enjoyed the enthusiasm that new auditors exhibit. They dig and dig until they find something and then that something becomes a big deal. It actually pains them when their manager shows them that it may not have the impact that the auditor thought it might. Over time we learn to balance the issue with the facts. Unfortunately, that balancing act sometimes does not include discernment.

The key to being able to discern is to control your emotions. The influence that emotion has over an auditor is measureable. It is evident in the tone of communication, personal appearance, and in thought processes.

Our jobs allow for a full range of emotions. Frustration, elation, anger, and satisfaction, as well as others, occur in almost every audit engagement. Most successful auditors can control them to some degree. However, to be the best, emotions must not impact your ability to discern the truth of the situation.

The third Key to Excellence is:

The more "out of the box" an auditor can be, the more flexible they become. That flexibility really translates into meaningful and actionable recommendations.

I remember that early in my career I was presented an opportunity to think outside the box and be flexible. I had just joined a credit risk review function for a large bank and was on my first assignment. After selecting the requisite sample of loans for review I diligently plodded through the pages and pages of file information to determine if they were underwritten to standard. I was about to wrap up that part of the audit when the head of credit risk review decided to pay the team a visit. Once he arrived, he decided he wanted to watch this new examiner in action. I certainly didn't want him to watch me reunderwrite consumer loans so I decided to interview several underwriters. That evening I drafted a list of interview questions and the next day, with my bosses boss in hand, began to do something that had not been done before.

The interviews went well and we actually found out things like workload, training, skills, file status upon first review, and how many times underwriters would look at the same file. Ultimately we ended up with several recommendations over the process of underwriting that would not have been discovered if we had only referred to a file review.

Several months later in a bank-wide conference for credit risk review, my bosses' boss reflected on his experience with me and informed his group that the practice of interviewing underwriters would now become part of the process for everyone.

It always amazes me how little things can often have big results. Funny, even today, many credit review functions do not interview underwriters during their examination process. Why is that?

The fourth Key to Excellence is:

Never allow your integrity to come under question.

Have you ever noticed how your client tries to manage your work? I had two interesting examples where the business client thought that they would prove themselves more adept at managing the audit than my team. The first example took place when the institution I was working for started to rate management's awareness of risks and control breaks. What that meant was that auditors had to assign an audit rating as well as a management awareness rating. It did not take long for management teams to create a work around. They would send a team of quality control experts to any areas we were going to audit about six months prior to our arrival. This team of experts would then provide management with a list of issues that needed to be addressed. Management would then start to address the issue and document that activity in an appropriate audit trail. In effect, management had created a preaudit audit.

Then, once the audit team arrived on site, management would provide the lead auditor with a breakdown of all known issues and action plan statuses, ensuring a high rating for management awareness. This happened to me twice though it happened to other auditors much more than that.

After a few reviews where management awareness ratings were less than satisfactory, my boss called and asked why we were having so many low scores. I told her the story of the preaudit audit and the representations of certain management teams. I also explained how I broke the spell. I simply asked management for the same document they provided my team at arrival but the one for the last four quarters.

When they didn't have that report, we all knew what was going to happen. Management had not established a sustainable control and therefore I could not allow that to continue. While I do not question the integrity of management in how they wanted to manage the rating, I do have to sleep at night. My own integrity meant that I had to call them on it and make a point.

The second example happened as I led a three-country audit. We followed the practice of sharing every issue with management as they surfaced and then resharing them two or three additional times throughout the rest of the engagement. By the time we held the exit meeting, no one could say that they were not aware of the issues. More importantly, they could not say that they did not have ample opportunity to debate the issue.

In this instance, management liked to use "the right people did not have time to discuss the issue" approach. In this approach, every local leader has plenty of time to review all issues. What really happens is the regional management team decides not to get involved until the closing conference. At that time, they would arrive at the exit meeting and begin to debate all the issues all over again. This debate would last until the auditor was so tired that they gave in. Ultimately it was a great strategy on behalf of management that historically brought them good results.

Being wise to this approach, I followed our process throughout the audit and scheduled the audit close for 11:00 a.m. on Friday morning. I then scheduled my plane back to the US for 2:00 p.m. that same afternoon. As the teams gathered in the conference room, I noticed some individuals who had not been present in any of our other meetings. I introduced myself and began the meeting.

This is what I said after thanking the president of the bank and his staff for all their support.

"You have received a copy of the report. You have all received the issues earlier and had the opportunity to respond to them. Nothing here should be a surprise to anyone. Typically, in this meeting, I like to focus on structuring the responses to the report and the issues because you will need to get those to me in fifteen business days. One thing that I do not do in this meeting is revisit any of the issues that have already been fully vetted with local management. If I have to do that, and sometimes it has happened, I just want to let you know that the overall rating will drop by one classification. If I miss my plane, which leaves at 2:00 p.m., the issues increase in severity." I smiled and we closed in fifteen minutes.

You will note that in each instance I did not get upset at why management did what they did. I did not let emotion drive my actions. I just let my intellectual integrity outshine theirs.

Now let's take a look at Keys to Excellence #5 and 6:

Always define terms and ensure full understanding before proceeding with your work.

Remember to "commune" with your clients. Drive to common understanding and definition, not just of words and printed material, but implied realities as well. This means you may need to change your perspective and that is all right.

Every audit team I have ever worked with has the same basic focus—improve the teams writing skills. Every regulator I have ever met always complains that auditors do not write well. They complain that issues are not clear; that reports are not appropriately detailed, and that work papers do not stand alone.

You know what? They are write. Excuse me, I mean they are right.

However they do miss one other salient point. Auditors typically don't communicate well verbally either. I remember one instance where my lead auditor was closing out an audit. During the meeting she told the business head that there was an issue in a certain area. This issue, she said, is there even if his management team tells him differently because *"she had worked in that area herself and the same problem existed back then as well."*

To the leaders' credit, he did not respond to that statement. About ten minutes later he asked to see me outside the conference room. We both excused ourselves, the meeting continued, and once outside he simply asked: "What does Mary have against me? Is there a hidden agenda here?" I assured him that she did not and that there was not. We went back into the room and finished the meeting but I knew that Mary had lost some respect from the business leader for her comment.

Communication is one of the most important aspects of an auditor's job. When discussing this topic with other audit leaders, I am often surprised by their perspective. Everyone says that it is important. Everyone says that they provide writing classes, negotiating and influencing, even presentation skills training. No one said they provided classes in improving communication.

Communication, commune, and community all have the same basic Latin root meaning: to make common. This implies that communication is more than a report or a meeting. It is more than providing information. It is more than receiving information. It is "to make common."

There was one audit that occurred in a collection shop of a large bank. The audit team was reviewing the MIS and management reporting. During the engagement, management assured the audit team that the right information was being sent to home office for their reporting to the regulators. The audit team was stymied because when looking at the local reporting, everything was done exactly as outlined by policy. When the team looked at home office reporting, everything was done exactly to policy. Yet the team could not reconcile the data in both reports to each other. After further investigation the source of the problem was found. One data element in each report was titled the same. However, the definition of each data element was different and contained a unique aspect that was not considered by the other. So while they each reported correct numbers, they were both incorrect.

I now make it a practice to ensure that I understand the definition of terms before arriving at any conclusion. It is an added step, but really pays dividends.

Because not all auditors have mastered these seven brand components, you are standing on the edge of greatness. By incorporating these seven traits or habits into your brand and balancing them with your own personality, you will create a successful brand that will propel you beyond the best.

Listening is Never Overrated

Have you ever watched auditors interviewing people or reporting out on findings? It fascinates me to sit back and watch one of my staff try to convince someone that what they have found and their interpretation of it is correct. Inevitably they all approach it the same way. It is almost as if they believe that if I do all the talking then the client cannot object. The best auditors do more than convince someone that their point of view is correct. They help their client convert themselves into believing what they are seeing. This conversion process relies on well-constructed facts that provide the pathway to conviction. That being said, our next "Key to Excellence (7)" is: *Arguments are more easily won if the other person convinces themselves of the facts, issues, or the resolution.*

Years ago, a team of auditors were in a foreign country. The audit of the pension fund company was progressing nicely with a few exceptions noted, but generally results were positive. One issue though took a little more communication than the others. It seemed that the business had decided to invest customer's retirement funds offshore in one of the parent company's investment vehicles. This made a lot of sense as the investment was more secure than onshore vehicles and the return was 200 bps higher than what a customer could obtain at home. From a business and customer centric view, the decision made good sense.

The local law however prohibited such investments. The law was quite specific and if found in noncompliance, an institution could face fines up to several million dollars. Aware of this law, the local business

11

obtained legal opinion from three local attorneys and one offshore attorney. The result of all of this legal expertise was that the business could continue to invest offshore without significant impact to its ability to comply with the local law.

The audit team reviewed all the data and after much internal discussion decided to elevate an issue regarding the process. Ultimately, the audit team determined that, notwithstanding the legal opinion, the practice could be determined to be in violation of the local law. As a result, the business was exposed to fines, censure, and a negative hit to their local reputation. When the issue was first surfaced, nearly all of management and audit leadership wanted to place value in the legal opinions and the fact that the customer was better off as mitigants to the risk of regulatory censure and/or fines.

The lead auditor to his credit decided to go against the grain and report the issue. However, he wanted to ensure that the president of the company understood how this auditor was assessing the risk and why it was going to be in the report.

The conversation was pleasant. The auditor indicated that he was not discounting the customer value, nor dismissing the legal opinions (regarding the latter, as an auditor you should always review legal opinions and not just accept on face value). His argument was very simple: There was a law on the books that was very clear which indicated that the practice the business was using was illegal. There was no exception to the law that would allow the argument that it was "in the customer's best interest." Because it is a violation of the law, the organization should be prepared to pay the resultant fines and perhaps even reserve money for that payment.

The president of the company was thoughtful and said he understood the auditor's point of view. He too knew the law did not allow for an exception but had counted on the customer value argument to dissuade regulators. However, the more he thought about it, and during the discussion, a light came on. "Perhaps," he said, "rather than an opinion from attorneys I should have talked to my friend in the regulatory body here to gauge his reaction to our argument. He may have given us special consideration. Now though, he might be in a public position where he cannot do that. I wish I had of thought of this first."

The auditor relaxed a bit as the president continued. "I think I will give him a call. At the worst, we will advise them before they find out about it themselves. What else do you think we should do?"

The auditor suggested that based on the results of the conversation, a reserve to pay the fine might make sense if revenue alone will not cover it. The president agreed. The auditor left the meeting with one last request. "By the way, would you give me a call and let me know how much the fine is going to be?" The auditor's smile was nearly as large as that of the president.

Six months later, a phone call, $2mm fine and a simple statement, "I think I should listen to you more often."

As an auditor you will want to be able to help your clients convince themselves that issues are issues and that solutions might work. Once committed to their own belief, the results of their actions will be much more meaningful.

Now, before we can get to the point of helping clients accept an issue, the auditor needs to listen. There are many classes on enhancing listening skills. Some teach you to learn certain techniques. For example, one is called "parroting" the question, i.e., "So let's see if I heard you correctly?" Another technique is taking copious notes and send an email confirming any agreements, or simply just nodding heads and thinking we communicated. While these may all work to some degree, to be the best auditor, this chapter's second "Key to Excellence (8)" is: *It is not enough to listen; one must learn what is being communicated.*

In my research for this chapter a sudden truth appeared. All these classes on enhancing listening skills do very little to help anyone listen. Aside from the money it provides, consultants and teachers, the vast majority of these courses provide superficial techniques to feign one's ability to listen. Let me explain why, and I will start with three simple definitions.

- Listen: to give attention with the ear, attend closely for the purpose of hearing.
- Hear: to perceive by the ear, to learn by the ear.
- Learn: to acquire knowledge of a skill by studying, instruction, or experience; to ascertain.

I really don't like definitions that include other words that then need to be defined. In these definitions, direct from the dictionary, to listen you have to hear. Because of that, as well as for other reasons, let us dismiss the definition of "Listen" and by default, also the term "listen" from our vocabulary.

The definition of "hear" seems to not go far enough. Perceive something and you might be right, learn something and you probably are right. You can learn to perceive so that your perception will help you learn. Seems a bit circuitous too me. Let's discount the term hear as well.

That leaves us with the term "learn." In my mind, if I replace listening with learning, I think I am better positioned to excel as an auditor.

In the audit process, we should be learning every day. However, many of us fall into the trap that when communicating I do not need to learn. I need to politely listen. I need to share ideas. I need to debate or argue, but certainly, heaven forbid communication is not a learning exercise. For that I read text books, I experience something, I go to IIA training classes. To be the best auditor though you have to realize that communication is all about learning!

Native Americans would listen to nature. They knew that if the wind blew a certain direction, specific weather would follow. They could hear a deer move in a forest as thick as a jungle because they learned what certain sounds meant. In many council meetings, only the chiefs would talk. The braves would listen because this was the way that they learned. Tribal history was often passed verbally from one generation to another and little, if anything, was ever lost. This art of <u>learning</u> <u>communication</u> seems to have disappeared. So how do we get it back and how does it apply to you?

Key to Excellence #9: *Study before you perform test work.*

It makes little sense in today's electronic and information age to learn about a business on the say you walk into their home office. Many auditors will have done their homework and read key articles, blogs, and magazine articles prior to departing for the first client meeting. The best auditor goes just a little bit further.

Year ago I was tasked with leading an audit on the bankruptcy processes of the bank that I worked for at that time. Honestly, I knew very little about bankruptcy but did know that it was important. I read what I could but just didn't get anything out of the ordinary from all of the information available. I have always had a healthy respect for studying, so I read, and read, and read. I felt though that there had to be a better way. Then an idea hit me.

What if I performed a walkthrough of a competitor's bankruptcy process? Was there anyone who might allow me and a couple of my staff to learn about managing bankruptcy? How much was proprietary? Would they be concerned re sharing secrets? The idea sounded great but the application of it was difficult, or so I thought.

As I thought through the dilemma I remembered that a couple of old friends of mine were now working for other institutions. One managed a collections shop in a bank and another worked in collections for a mortgage company. I gave them both a call. Within a week, my team of three was in both Pittsburg and Des Moines walking through two different organizations' bankruptcy shops and learning a lot about how to manage the risks associated with bankruptcy. When we finally arrived on site of our own audit, the team had the confidence and knowledge to perform a great audit.

Sometimes study takes shape in activities not related to reading books or attending training classes. The best auditors learn to think outside the box, utilize all their resources, and ultimately make the best impressions with the quality of their work.

Key to Excellence #10: *Try something out before you audit (do-through) don't just perform a walkthrough.*

A standard tool for all auditors is to perform a process walkthrough. While these may take several different shapes, typically a walkthrough is when an auditor walks through a process by talking with all the people who perform tasks associated with that specific process. A lot of knowledge can be gathered by talking with the people who actually perform the tasks being reviewed. This process has standard application and each audit team I worked with used it to good success. Needless to say, the auditors learned a lot about a process by talking with each participant and sometimes watching what they do.

One day during a staff meeting, one of my auditors mentioned that they had a concern. They were performing a walkthrough of an application approval process and when talking with one of the employees he became confused. It seemed that his conversations with management regarding the process and his view of the process being effectuated were different. On a lark he asked the person he was with if they would mind if he, the auditor, actually performed the function. Where upon the employee said absolutely not a problem. My auditor changed seats and after learning the process as directed by the employee, my auditor began to perform the function according to the way that management told him it was being done. The processes were different so the auditor asked the employee why they were not performing their function according to management's expectation. The employee showed the auditor that the system would not allow certain steps to occur so she had developed a manual work around. When asked if management knew about the system problem, the auditor was told that they did but that they not want to fix it. She also said that there were several other "tricks" that the team had developed because the system was not supportive of the processes that had been designed.

A simple walkthrough may not have caught this divergence between process and action, but performing the function prompted a more detailed conversation. Ultimately the system was upgraded to perform the processes as designed and manual processes were eliminated.

Key to Excellence #11: *Seek knowledge from those who know through inquiry (your circle of counselors).*

I have always kept a group of close friends close to me. These friends are not the ones I go to ball games with or have dinner with all the time. Our families don't see each other on the weekends and our kids don't go to school together. They could, but they don't.

No, these friends are my business circle of influence. They are experts in products, processes, risks, or controls and from time to time I reach out to them. Usually I reach out to them while in the heat of the audit engagement because I want to ensure that what I am being told is accurate. About fifteen years ago I found that a better use of their time, and another little something that set me apart from my peers, was to interview my circle during the planning of my audit. These outside experts then became integral in my learning about the risks and controls associated with whatever I was auditing. At a minimum they confirmed my understanding of certain aspects of an organization/process/risk or, in the best of cases, educated me on what I should really be focused on and why that focus was important.

Each interview became a work paper and the knowledge I gained helped me to scope my audits. While many auditors probably talk to someone during planning, the following lists might help you who want to be the best auditors achieve that dream.

Circle of Influence Membership: (include these people if you can)

A regulator: (FRB, FDIC, OCC) I would recommend one from each branch and be sure to include compliance, stress testing, credit, and technology experts in your group.
An external consultant: Not someone who charges for everything but someone with whom you can exchange information and they can provide expert opinion.

A quant: A lot of models and data management in use so it pays to have someone close.

A systems programmer: They can give you the real scoop.

A risk manager: Their perspective is a real plus.

An attorney: Who can't use an attorney?

A CEO: If you really want to know what is important to a business leader.

An audit manager of a competing firm: Provide another perspective on impact.

A treasury specialist:

A broker:

An insurance specialist:

A mechanic: There are no better process people who know what connects to what.

A successful waiter/waitress: Who better to handle objections?

An artist: For an alternative point of view.

A review of the list will surprise some of you. Many will laugh at the last three entries. However, if you really want to be the best, you need to have alternative points of view provided to you. Experts in other fields than yours can provide that point of view. Remember, many companies went to Disney Land to learn customer service even though none of them had amusement parks. It is not wrong to seek expertise everywhere, it is only wrong not to seek it.

Key to Excellence #12: *Don't opine until you have enough information upon which to base an opinion.*

One of the most consistent events that occur during an audit is arriving at a conclusion. Unfortunately, these conclusions arrive way too early in the process. Eighty percent of audit conclusions occur after one test, one walkthrough, or one conversation. Auditors are so anxious to prove their worth that they quickly arrive at a final position even if they have not completed the test work. Or worse, they complete the test work with the end already in mind. Either way is wrong.

In law, particularly in criminal investigations, you are taught to let the evidence lead you to your conclusion. This is good advice for the best auditor as well. There is nothing wrong with contemplating several possible outcomes of any situation. Don't allow yourself to fall into the trap of concluding after one test and then making an opinion. Your opinion should be based on more than one event or one conversation. There will come a time during the process, and quite naturally, where the preponderance of the information, will lead you to the right conclusion.

Key to Excellence #13: *Don't judge intent of words, seek to understand them (ask follow-ups or confirm your understanding of what is meant).*

Have you ever noticed that in the English language certain words have multiple meanings? Take the word "duck." You can use it in the following sentences: I shot a duck yesterday when I went hunting. Also: To miss the ball thrown my way I had to duck quickly. This is a simple but excellent example of how a single word may have more than one meaning. Obviously, as we read the two preceding sentences it is easy to tell the difference and know how the word "duck" is being used. All words are not so easily understood.

Also, emotion plays a significant role in how we interpret the meaning of a word. Take the word "love." I love chocolate ice cream. I love that song. I love my mother. In the heat of passion, when one says "I love you," the recipient often hears a completely different word than when the same word "Love" is used to express pride or to soothe hurt feelings like, "But you know I love you."

Because it is hard to decipher the meaning or the tone of the word, auditors often have to struggle and determine the meaning of certain words or combination of words.

I was being examined by our friendly regulators. They were looking at our new audit process and in an interview they asked me how I felt our team was doing. Being the ever transparent person and believing that this examiner knew that I had set high standards for myself and my team, I confided that I felt we were about 65 percent of the way there. I then explained that good progress has been made but some of the team was struggling with the new process so it will take a little longer to get to a point where I would be happy. I also pointed out that no risks are being left on the table. At the close of the examination we were not rated as high as we had hoped. One of the reasons was that the examiner stated that because I, as chief auditor was not happy with our progress, then he as an examiner could not be either. The examiner failed to consider my high standards and did not consider the risk exposure that was or was not evident as a result of our "not being there." The lesson to me was to not opine on how we are doing, just ensure that whoever asks the questions gets the complete answer before they leave the room.

To avoid misunderstanding and arrive at faulty conclusions, each of us must be confident that we understand the meaning of and the emotion behind words used by our clients.

Key to Excellence #14: *Clarification is not a sign of weakness. Make sure that you understand the context. In other words, know the reasons behind the answers.*

Very much aligned with Key to Excellence number 11 is this secret. Not only do we need to be sure of the definition of a key word and the emotion behind it, auditors must ensure that the context is well understood. Clarification helps us get to that point.

I have to admit I am not a fan of the tried and true clarification process professional consultants have taught us. I find it unusual to say to someone, "Let me make sure I understand what you just said" or "If I hear you correctly you said . . ." Those phrases make either me or my client think one of us is not very smart. Usually it is not my client.

A good alternative to the above mentioned approaches might be something like the following: "That is very interesting, Bill. So when you perform this reconciliation process between data provided from customer service to the data provided credit, you actually created an algorithmic approach to it. Could you walk me through how that algorithm works?"

You get to the same point and have confirmed (or allowed the client to correct your understanding) exactly what the client said without putting in question his or your sanity or intellect.

If I don't understand something I quickly admit it and simply say: "That sounds great, Bill, unfortunately I don't quite understand why you have to transfer radioactive waste on rail cars through big cities like Chicago."

Another good technique is to ask the client why they think the way that they do. For example, there is nothing wrong with asking the head of credit why he/she believes that vintage analysis has limited application to credit card portfolio management. An auditor doesn't just want an answer they should want the reasons behind the answer.

Key to Excellence #15: *Hear what is not said and apply it to your learning.*

One of the basic strategies that management uses tin dealing with auditors is that they only answer the questions that auditors ask. I have heard management say things as directly as "Only answer that the auditor asks and don't tell them anything more. If they don't know to ask then that is their problem."

This puts a lot of responsibility on the shoulders of the auditor. The questions asked now have to de designed to get all the facts. Even in the best of cases the auditor may still not have the whole picture. That is why it is important for auditors to learn to hear what is *not* being said.

Years ago I was working for a large international financial institution that had just rolled out a self-assessment process. Internal audit management decided that if the business had adopted and implemented the new self-assessment processes then they would be given credit for knowing their issues, and if they were working to resolve them, then they would be given credit for that as well.

Needless to say, almost every business we went into during that time provided us a list of known issues and an expectation that any issues audit reported would not negatively affect the "Management Awareness Rating," unless it was an issue that was not on the working self-assessment issue list.

After two or three audits, where no additional issues were found by internal audit, a friend of mine told me that management had implemented a process where about six months prior to the audit of any area, a special team would review that area and elevate to the business group all potential issues. The management team then presented that list of issues to the auditors as the results of their self-assessment process. With this new information, we began asking management how long they had known about the issues that they presented in their list. Answers would vary but mostly business management would not answer the question at all rather redirect the auditor to the list at hand and the work that was being done to address the issues. The audit team began to listen to those nonanswers and armed with the additional information began to arrive at different conclusions.

I don't know about you but I am not a big fan of this type of process. I instructed my team to accept the list of known issues when management gave it to them but with a slight variable. I wanted the same list for six, nine, and twelve months prior to our visit. That way my audit team could support the sustainability of this new self-assessment process that management was so excited about. Needless to say, there were no other reports. As a result, the audit team gave credit to management for having a list of issues but criticized them for lack of a sustainable self-assessment process.

Management's practice of pre-empting the audit team ended shortly thereafter.

Key to Excellence #16: *Don't be afraid to communicate what you really see. Debate is a healthy part of listening.*

Have you ever thought that your managers' editing of your issue and/or your report was wasteful? After spending hours crafting your written product, someone reviews it and change the words, the meaning and sometimes, even the tone. As you sit there reading it, and once the initial angst subsides, you note that the rewrite actually is more reflective of your issue than what you wrote. You quickly wonder why that happens and attribute it to the managers' experience, and then move on to the next project.

To be the best you can be you may want to analyze why someone can gather facts and write something completely different than the person who performed the work and originally presented the facts. Let's explore that for just a moment.

Not long ago I was working with a client. During the planning of the audit, the team noted a potential significant issue and approached management about it. During the discussions it was decided that rather than complete and audit in order to elevate the issue, a task force, including internal audit, would be formed to resolve the issue. The task force went to work, progress was made, and internal audit wrote an audit memo to close out the exercise.

When management reviewed a draft of the memo and wanted to make some edits. They wanted to get credit for work previously done as well as acknowledging the recent work of the task force. I asked them, what it was that they actually had done, just in case I had missed something.

Management began by telling us that they had been aware of the issue for almost two years. They had discussed the issue in several meetings and amongst themselves. They were almost ready to resolve the concerns but had to postpone everything until after a system conversion. They wanted to make sure that senior management was aware of all those facts.

I simply asked them, "Are you sure?"

So I rewrote the audit memo with this new information. I highlighted that management had been aware of the potential issue for almost two years. I noted, quite eloquently if I do say so myself, that they even discussed the issue at several meetings. Then I pointed out that even with this foreknowledge and discussion, nothing had been done to address the issue until internal audit elevated it.

I presented the revised draft of the memo to the business leadership team. They were not happy. I explained to them that I am willing to highlight what they wanted highlighted but I have an obligation to point out the inaction that actually took place. I cannot report half of the facts without sharing the rest of the story too. To make a long story short, and after a few more minutes of debate, we published the original memo.

Being able to communicate what I saw, beyond what they thought I saw, allowed us to be more balanced in our finalization of the project. It also afforded me the opportunity to educate the team on how internal audit defines "did something."

Key to Excellence #17: *Listen without prejudice. In other words, do not prejudge what you are about to hear. Listen to understand, not to assess judgment.*

From time to time television presents some very good series. They are entertaining, professionally done, and provide some personal insights as part of the delivery. I know that we all have seen those moments that we automatically relate to either our personal lives or to our work environment. *Ally McBeal* was one such series.

I enjoyed the show because of the music and the lawyering and the interplay between all the characters. I often said that if I could find a law firm like Cage and Fish, I would have been a lawyer.

There were also many hidden gems scattered throughout the different episodes. For example, in one episode, Alley is talking with her roommate Renee who was struggling with a weekly personal struggle. In the process of that struggle, Renee turns to Ally for advice. Ally, ever the attorney, asked her friend, "Do you want my advice or do you just want me to just listen?" (sic)

I perked up a bit when I heard that question. Quickly I realized that there is a significant difference between listening to hear and listening to provide advice. The difference is not always in the question or supporting arguments, but more in the recipients posturing to provide a service. When we listen to provide advice, we are already formulating our advice as the person is speaking to us. We hear what helps us construct our own response and sometimes fail to notice subtle comments that would have an impact to our response.

On the other hand, when we listen to hear, we are not forming any kind of response. We do not have a preconceived idea of how the answer might go because we are not expecting ourselves to answer anything about what we have just heard. In this case, Ally listened and gave her friend a hug and said that everything would work out okay.

Auditors too often go to interviews with preconceived ideas. They then design questions to support those ideas and prove to themselves that they were correct. In the course of some of those interviews, auditors ignore answers that do not meet their expectations. Don't be one of those auditors. The best auditors know how to listen, to hear, and to understand.

Thinking is the Auditors Best Friend

A man is but the product of this thoughts, what he thinks, he becomes.
—Mahatma Gandhi

I often tell my staff that the audit profession is a thinking person's profession. If you don't want to think then don't come here and work for me. Many of my peers agree although they may say it differently. Statements like "I don't want any checklist auditors on my staff"; "I need analysts who can think on my staff!" or "I wish I had some creative talent on my team because we need to find new ways to audit." Everyone desires the same skill and that skill is the ability to think.

As an industry we are met with many expectations. As a group we are evolving and the audit process is changing. However, I have noted that for all the attempts, all the leadership focus, all the desires and willingness to move forward, we don't seem to be making much progress. Part of the reason we have not advanced as far as we probably should have is that this thinking thing is uncomfortable. In fact, Henry Ford once said, "Thinking is the hardest work there is, which is probably the reason so few engage in it."

If thinking is the hardest work there is, why is it that we do so little of it in audit? Is it because we are so focused on the audit plan, completing the audit, meeting deadlines, and moving to the next assignment, that we rush through work? The audit gets completed but at what cost to the individual auditor?

Honestly, most audit teams do a good job of auditing. They design good tests. They perform interviews, process walkthroughs, and complete test work with great ability. Even so, many clients don't believe that auditors do enough. They don't believe in the value that is being provided. As an auditor who wants to go beyond the best make sure that you do not lose the ability to think.

If we have the ability to think, and trust me not all of us do, then we have to ensure that we have time to practice this skill. I have always tried to schedule "thinking" time into our audit plans. Then, we do the same in each audit. This is a bit difficult because you really want to take advantage of working hours to be with your client and completing required test work. With that in mind, thinking time usually occurs after work hours. We schedule at least one hour every day during fieldwork for "thinking" time. At first the team always looks upon this idea with some skepticism. They wanted to go home after a hard day in the trenches. Some had obligations of school or family. Others just needed to get away from it all.

However, once one auditor tried taking the time to think, the rest of the team started to see the value of that one extra hour a day. As the quality of work improved for the one auditor, others began to set up "thinking" time as well. Before long, the majority of staff was spending more time thinking and ultimately the audits improved, time was better managed, and clients could see real value in the work provided.

It isn't easy. Thinking takes practice and like anything, baseball, skiing, macramé; it takes dedication. It also means that we need to break some bad habits. For example:

Key to Excellence #18: *Don't do checklist auditing.*

Have you ever wondered why so many Big 4 and financial auditing consultants use checklists? When asked, they respond that it helps facilitate the audit and drives consistency. While both of those might be true, what it really does is to force auditors to produce audit after audit, quickly, efficiently, and *profitably*. It also helps document tasks that were performed. In the rush to process uniformity, we have forgotten that a checklist was originally used to "jog the memory." In other words, a checklist is supposed to help us remember to do certain things. It was never meant to be that thing we were supposed to remember to do. Yet we have become so use to checklists that even the businesses perform some of their work via this overused tool. The best auditors use checklist for the right purpose. They do not let the checklist become the purpose.

Key to Excellence #19: *Don't let the first answer be the right answer, unless it is.*

The best auditors will never allow the first answer to be the only or the surest answer. Facts presented always tell more than one story. The more the facts the more of the story one can determine. The more that the facts are verified the more valid the story becomes. Many times, the first answer is only the first answer. Very seldom is that answer the "right" one!

The following poem presents a humorous look at this exact situation.

The Issue

She'd finally done it, yes indeed
she'd found the one in record speed.
This issue is so big, she sighed,
that Pete and Jack and Dan will cry!

She'd found the one, that sacred grail
the great example of a "fail."
So big a deal all will proclaim
and shout Hosanna's to her name!

This issue is the one that sings
it is the only one with wings.
It touches all important risks,
points to controls that don't exist!

This issue, yes this omnibud
more powerful than an errant scud,
will make the business cringe with fear
and to the regulator become endeared.

And so this morning just as planned
towards the office, issue in hand,
she sat in front of Daniel's desk
ready for the coming test.

Dan slowly read the issue twice
(She thought this meant that it was nice)
Then set the paper on his desk
And with a smile he did profess . . .

"I am not sure I understand
the problem with the bathroom fan.
And while I get the work you did,
I do not see it quite this big!"

"Perhaps you should go back and see
if there is more that you can bring to me.
Because without substantive proof,
we have no case, we have no truth!"

Her eyes turned down, her smile was done
She felt a failure, her job was gone
But just as feelings beyond repair
engulfed her soul with grim despair
Dan smiled and said this simple phrase
"I like the way you wrote it."

Her joy returned, she felt renewed
She knew what she had left to do
Some analytics, a test or three
And then he'd love it, just wait and see.

> And then this issue would become
> The mega issue . . .
> A Priority 1.

While the poem takes a lighthearted look at audit issues, the point that we should not lose is that sometimes the first answer is not the right answer. Sometimes we have to go further and think through alternative potential answers to get to the right conclusion. The best auditors question the first answer until they are sure that it is the right answer.

Key to Excellence #20: *Ask others on the team for their opinions.*

I have been in many audits and worked with many teams. I remember that on one occasion I had the opportunity to work with and experienced and well-respected audit lead. This person was well known for asking the team's opinion and engaging each team member in the audit. I was told that I could learn a lot from this person.

I was excited to get started. I wanted to learn the secrets of team management and engagement so I watched every step this lead auditor took. It was exciting to watch how this person engaged different team members at different points of the audit. I was fascinated by the way she leveraged the skills of her team and obtained insights from members about what they knew best. I was intrigued by her ability to translate their opinions into her own decisions. She made sure that every opinion mattered. Auditors loved working with her because they knew that she respected them and what they could bring to the table.

I finished the audit and thought through the experience. I then had lunch with my lead and asked her why she spent so much time soliciting the input of team members when her own experience was so vast that she could probably do the job without any of us. Her answer was simple and direct. "Dan," she said, "my experience is only my experience. When I have a team I need to learn from them and their experiences. That way, my own experience grows with each audit. Honestly, I don't think I could do it any other way."

"But it takes so much time, and you always have different opinions. Doesn't that take up too much time?" I asked.

"Yes, it is time consuming. But it is worth it. The extra few hours a week I put in to learn from the team helps me think through the audit. Once I have all the facts and the different opinions, I can think through how I am going to present our concerns. Without the opinions of the team, I am not sure that I have enough to think about. That means I would get to the wrong conclusions."

I learned from a lot from watching her and working with her. And now, I too take the extra time to ask my team's opinions as I am thinking through the audit.

Key to Excellence #21: *Seek the advice of your circle of influence.*

The value of thinking manifests itself in many ways. Ultimately the value is equal to the process developed to help us think. Some of us will read and contemplate. Others will discuss what we are thinking to receive affirmation of our thought process. We all have a thinking process. Our process is developed as we grow and is based on a lot of factors. Our education, our work experiences, our home life, and our friends all play a part in our thinking process.

Attorneys learn to think a certain way. Accountants think another way. Politicians, when they do think, think differently yet. Philosophers and religious leaders think differently too. There is nothing wrong with developing a process to think. The challenge is to leverage the different thinking processes available so that your conclusions are sound. The best way to leverage these diverse thinking processes is to make sure that you take advantage of your "circle of influence." If you have constructed the proper circle of influence, you will reap the benefits of diverse thought processes.

I want to share a couple of tips on how to best leverage your circle of influence. When seeking advice make sure that you have defined the situation clearly. The more clarity there is the easier it will be to apply expertise in the form of advice. Not only that, you will also be better able to explore or flex your follow-up questions so that the focus does not expand to the periphery.

Also, be prepared. Never cold call your circle of influence. Your relationship with your circle is a professional one, not a social one. Twitter, Instagram, and the like are your social outlets. This is a working relationship that you have created to help you be better at what you do. By planning your calls and meetings, you stay true to that premise and show respect to each member of your circle.

Key to Excellence #22: *Don't be an auditor who cannot think.*

It may sound harsh, but today you just cannot afford to associate with old-fashioned audit traditionalists. These traditionalists espouse the use of checklists, support the raising of every observation as an issue, and generally can't move beyond the weeds in any audit engagement. You know some of these traditionalists. You probably have worked with them. They may have audited you. You probably are quick to share their weaknesses to anyone who will listen. Unfortunately, sometimes we fall into the same category without even recognizing it. Let me give you an example.

During the recent financial crisis, many smaller-sized banks and a few large ones as well failed. They were taken over by the regulators or merged with other larger banks. Obviously there was a lot of finger pointing going around and no one was absent some of the guilt.

An interesting aspect to this crisis was the limited criticism of banks audit departments. Of course there were some instances where regulators were critical, but for the most part, internal audit came out of the crisis no worse for the wear. Unless of course you take a critical eye to this situation and realize the catastrophic dearth of thoughtful auditing that occurred that contributed to the crisis.

Many audit teams perform several tasks for an institution. One of those tasks for banks is performing compliance to Sarbanes Oxley requirements, or otherwise known as SOX testing. Did you know that in the vast majority of all failed institutions, their SOX audit results were stellar? *No issues reported.*

I don't know about you but I cannot for the life of me rationalize why audit teams refer to the successful SOX testing process as a measurement of their success. I was hired by a bank that had its own troubles during that time. When I got there, the head of the SOX audit unit spend a lot of time telling me how great the audit of Sarbanes Oxley was. I asked a simple question, "If your audit process is so good why did we receive a Memorandum of Understanding from the regulators? Something must be missing from that exercise. What do you think the missing ingredient is?" There was silence and ultimately no response to that question at all.

We continued to conversation and I pointed out how some of the results of SOX testing actually indicated weak processes in other parts of the organization. I asked why those items were not followed up on and explored to see if there were problems. The answer was that there was no time as there were other SOX tests to complete. I arrived at the conclusion that the present audit team did not know how to take time to think about what the results told them. Rather than do that, they allowed themselves to rejoice in the satisfactory SOX results.

How many organizations do you know that believe a SOX audit is the best thing that has happened to the audit profession? This author believe s that SOX auditing is the worst thing that has happened to audit in over thirty years. Not that controls over financial reporting are not important. They are! Rather, SOX auditing reinforces the traditionalist's view of auditing. So time consuming is SOX auditing that audit teams do not have time or resources to pursue meaningful and impactful audit engagements. The other "truth" about SOX auditing is the primary fallacy of the regulation to begin with. You cannot regulate morality, which is what SOX tries to do. So now we have rules trying to control amoral behavior and as a result relegate the audit department to a group of mini CPAs running around looking for a few dollars here or there instead of big issues that contribute to huge problems. Problems, say, like the financial crisis that we just experienced.

Key to Excellence #23: *Don't Overthink!*

The final secret in this section is simply to not overdo it. In researching this section, I came upon the following quote.

Most of the problems in life are because of two reasons: We act—without thinking—or we keep thinking without acting.

—anonymous

Enough said.

Designing Team Success

You can do what I cannot do. I can do what you cannot do. Together we can do great things.
—Mother Teresa

Teamwork is what makes us successful. This is not a new concept. It is something that every audit department strives to master. It is hard to create that excellent team. It is hard to be, as an individual, the perfect teammate. In this chapter we will explore how to create team success by being the best teammate you can be.

I have had the pleasure of working with two really great teams. I have to admit that I was not the leader of either of these great teams but worked as an integral member of the team. In my analysis of these teams, I compared them to other teams I had belonged to earlier. It was eye opening to know the difference between very good and excellent. It was not much. Let me explain.

The first excellent team was found in Mexico. I worked for a large financial institution that had bought a large bank in the country. The new audit leader was constructing a team of auditors for that bank. This team would include some legacy Mexican auditors as well as a few "imports" from the new bank. I was lucky enough to be one of those new imports.

The first few months were not pretty and certainly we were not a very good team at first. But we all worked hard and slowly you could feel things change. Then one day, about a year and a half after we started, you just "felt" that the team had somehow jelled. We did in fact cross over from good to great. And for the following year we did some of the best auditing that the bank in Mexico had ever seen.

So what happened? Besides the fact that we all got comfortable with each other, the processes required and the philosophy of the audit leader, there were three key actions taken that pushed us over the edge towards great team history.

Key to Excellence #24: *Replace individual ego with team success.*

Vince Lombardi once said: "Individual commitment to a group effort—that is what makes a team work, a company work, a society work, a civilization work." Our group of individuals became a team when once we realized that our individual position and opinion was not as important as the team's position or opinion.

For several months each of us tried to posture ourselves as the most influential member of the team. No one was overly sneaky about it, but everyone had their one little trick they would use. It was fun to watch and participate in it until we realized that we were not making the progress that we needed to make.

Our leader was astute and held an off-site session for all of us. Most of the session has been forgotten but there was one activity that still stands out.

Our consultant was hired to help us become more like a team. We did not climb a mountain, or ford a river. What we did instead was to try and determine what each individual brought to the team and then why that team was better because of it.

The consultant asked all of us to think what kind of boat, within a flotilla, we each were. You know a yacht, a tanker, a barge, a speedboat, etc.? Then we had to determine what boat type we were and what type our teammates were. Then as a group we would agree on a type.

At the end it was deemed that I was a speed boat. The team saw me as someone who was a little faster than others, had the confidence to go fast, liked to stay away from the rest of the team and not be slowed down. While that can be looked at in the negative, the consultant actually turned it into a positive.

He asked me how could I use the "speed boat" image to help the team. We all brainstormed for a while and came up with some great ways to use my natural tendencies to help the team but maintain my individual personality. In other words, he helped the team use my strengths by showing me how to use my strengths to help the team.

As we each went through the exercise, we realized that there was nothing wrong with our differences and that each difference was really strength. All we had to do was let each person use that strength and watch as the team got better. The "Ah-ha" moment hit us all at the same time. It was fantastic. We all became a team that day because we realized that we lost nothing of ourselves by becoming a team.

Shortly thereafter, audit results in all phases of the job were excellent.

The Harmony of Team Work—Unifying Diverse Cultures and Creating the Best You

Recently I searched YouTube for videos of an oldie called "What Becomes of the Broken Hearted." There are several versions floating around, including the original Motown one with Jimmy Ruffin which is the one I remembered. I listened to the remake by Joan Osborne and after fifty times I realized that this version was even better than the original.

I then began to explore why I arrived at that conclusion. Here was a group of diverse people, coming together to sing a song, written over thirty years ago. True, the backup band included many of the original backup bandmates but the background singers and Joan were obviously new. As I listened and listened, I was able to determine why this video is an example of perfect harmony and teamwork.

Joan's voice is perfectly aligned to the gritty theme of the song and to the sound of Motown. She begins the song with pleasure in her smile and strength in her voice. Halfway through she becomes mesmerized and mesmerizing. This moment does not occur very often but you can clearly see it happen to her as she emerges herself completely in the moment.
While she is the lead, the background vocalists are just as important. Perfect pitch and timing, and when the camera turns to them, you can easily note the commitment they have to their parts and to the song in general. They do not over stage the lead singer but provide complete and complimentary support. As a result the song would not be the same without them and Joan's lead would be just another good song.

Scoping out the musicians, what a group you have: a keyboardist with a magicians hat, another with a backwards ball cap, two percussionists, plenty of guitars, brass, and a bass player. There is even a xylophonist. Each of them is focused on the moment and contributing their best to this song. I challenge anyone to actually "hear" the xylophone. Can you imagine what it must feel like to play an instrument that no one will even hear? Yet he is there throughout the entire song.

If you notice the twin drummers you will see that at times they are in perfect harmony. At other times they are playing in lock step but not perfectly aligned. To me, it seems to say that it is okay to have your own role within the sub role of the song.

As the end of this, I arrived at the conclusion that every piece has to be at its absolute best to provide such musical perfection. There is no room for egos or for one-ups-man-ship. Everyone dedicated to the song and the moment that they are enjoying.

I relate this little story because during the life of any organization, the people of that organization are introduced to new members. These members bring with them their own personal and corporate identities that can impact historic cultures and cause concern. I find it interesting that historic lessons are quickly forgotten when the lesson impacts us directly.

If an organizational culture that does not evolve and grow becomes stagnant and ultimately dies off, why would we not apply that to ourselves as well? The influx of new ideas and perspectives, of different success styles will only serve to make us better. I fully understand that there is fear in change. The fear of change is understandable but should not be acceptable, at least not if you want to be better than the best.

If we are not perceptive enough to realize the benefits of diversity of thought and culture we will not reach the pinnacle of success that can be achieved. We will not have the opportunity to witness Joan Osborne and "What's Become of the Broken Hearted."

It is said that after that performance, Joan simply asked, "What just happened?" Obviously she had recognized that this was a special session filled with magic. Her reaction was based on the totality of the experience and not just on her part. She really sensed that all the pieces came together at the right time. So while she was happy with her own performance, she enjoyed the effect that the whole production had on everyone. That is why this recording is so significant.

Key to Excellence#25: *Relish your teammate's success.*

It is literally true that you can succeed best and quickest by helping others to succeed.

—Napoleon Hill

This is an interesting statement. I remember early in my corporate career I was not so convinced that helping anyone else would do anything for me personally. I was in sales and rewarded by the number of deals I would make. My goal was to always beat my competitor, whether they worked for my company or not, into submission. I was good at it. I set several state records for sales and made few friends. I honestly didn't care.

My bosses thought that my success as a salesperson would transfer into management so they promoted me to my own office. So I moved to Arlington Texas and began the next phase of my corporate career. Our office was effectively located in a suburb of Dallas. The company had a large office in Dallas with three times as many employees as mine. But imagine this. After only six months we were out pacing the Dallas staff in sales. That's right. Six months. This success made me even more self-centered even though I would say it was my team. Frankly without me, the team had done nothing, and now with me? We were now number one.

This didn't last long. Once the deals dried up, as they always do, I found out who my true supporters were and there weren't many. My arrogance and focus on myself had eliminated any vestige of friendship and I was all alone. When I was moved into the "penalty box" for a number awhile it was time to take a hard look at myself and see what I needed to do to change.

Change is never easy. Sometimes it is good that we get older because as we age wisdom, seems to come out of nowhere to accompany us. At this time I started reading a lot of books about success. Every book I read, and I do mean every book, defined success as something that is not achieved alone. This was really very eye opening to me. In other words, my success never was really mine. It wasn't all about me.

As I recalled those productive months I suddenly realized that my office was full of people who helped us set those sales records and exceed production of the larger Dallas Office. Without any one of the other sales people not closing their deals, we would not have done it. The support staff was just as valuable because without them taking care of customers and paper work the rest of us would not have had time to sell. It truly was a team effort. How blind of me to not have noticed.

I decided to change my own definition of success. It was not really important or not whether anyone else did, but I knew I had to make the change. As I moved out of the "penalty box" and back into the good graces of management, it was a new me that emerged.

Twenty-eight years later after staying with the same company I think I learned my lesson.

For me, it is gratifying to see my staff come up with the big issue, or make a great recommendation and receive accolades from management. To see young people come into the group and make real contributions to the team is much more exciting to me. If I can help them achieve their goals then I know that the team will be successful.

A good demonstration of this is found in the movie *The Gladiator*. True, this is a story but all stories are based on belief. There is a scene where the gladiators have arrived in Rome and they are in the Colosseum. The day's event was designed to replicate the battle of Carthage which the Roman Army quite decidedly won. Into the arena marched the twenty gladiators. Shortly thereafter incomes the Roman chariots in their entire splendor. After a few passes by the chariots, the star of the show told the gladiators that they will only win if they work together, and not alone. Most of the team united and as the few stragglers were mowed down by the chariots one begins to see the effect that good teamwork can have. Ultimately, the gladiators triumph and history is rewritten, at least for one day.

Now, it is true that movies are not real. They do take liberties and this event probably never happened. But the message is true. You see the same thing happen in sports. Teams that are full of superstars don't often make it to the finals and if they do, how many times are they beaten by a team of players who don't make as much money, who don't have the prestige and probably has no superstars? It happens quite a lot. The Kansas City Royals are just one example of that.

The very same thing happens in audit. You have all seen it. There are teams that work well together, others that seem to have conflict. Then there are those rare occasions where magic happens. It is hard to explain, and very hard to define, but you know it is there because you feel it. I have been blessed to have that "magic" twice in my career. Both times it lasted for about twelve months. We could never describe it but we all knew that we were experiencing something special. As I look back on those experiences, there were a couple of common threads. One: we were all thrown together by circumstance. None of the team arrangements were naturally evolving or expected. And two: it was always us against the world. This latter idea is intriguing. I am not saying that we felt we had to beat the world, we just felt that the only people who would support us, help us, or give us credit was ourselves. We learned to relish each person's singular "victory" because we knew it was a team victory. Everyone helped everyone else be successful. There was no thought of ever going it alone. Some people had to pull back while others had to step up. But the team did exactly what was needed. And as a result, they were immensely successful.

Key to Excellence#26: *Always be positive in the face of adversity, especially in front of your team.*

The audit profession is one that deals with a lot of adversity. Some auditors have mastered the ability to defray adversity through humor. Other let it bother them for some period of time before finally letting go. And still others quite simply just ignore it. All of these approaches are fine if they work for you.

The best auditors though, confront adversity with positive resolution and demonstrate to team members exactly how to move forward. This ability is not easily obtained and it usually begins with simple steps. For example, if your team arrives at a remote site for an audit and all of a sudden you realize that one member is sick and cannot work. This puts you down one person and you still have a set time to complete the work. Some auditors would bemoan the fact that they lost a resource and immediately pick up the phone to ask for more time to complete the audit.

Other auditors would know that they would get no additional time and immediate start looking for a last second replacement, verbally decrying the situation that they are in and thereby making everyone on the team uncomfortable.

Still others would reduce audit scope while complaining that the audit will not be as effective or impactful as it could have been.

The best auditors take a different approach all together. Rather than say or react negatively to the situation, the best auditor will call the team together and let them know of the situation. As a team they will explore alternatives to replacing the work that was assigned but no longer will be completed. As they review, the team does reduce scope, but only by selective reduction of tests and utilizing alternative audit tools to complete others. The team involvement generates energy for the assignment and the team volunteers to work the extra hours needed to complete the task.

A positive attitude is invigorating for a team and seeing that someone knows how to approach a problem or setback constructively often ensures great audit results.

Now on to some specifics on how to construct your team when you are a leader.

Key to Excellence #27: *Don't replace the person, replace the skills, or better yet, add new skills to the team.*

When you are lucky enough to obtain a position where you must manage a team and have to replace a valued member by hiring new auditors, please don't make the mistake most every audit manager or director does. Don't think about replacing the person who has left. You can't. You will not replace the positive contributions the previous person made to your team. You will not be able to replace the weaknesses that person had either. And in all reality you will not be able to replace the skills the exiting staff member takes with them. Granted, you may be able to replace technical skills and perhaps even improve upon the previous level.

Most managers look to replace one skill set with the same, only improved, skill set. The best audit managers take a moment to look at the entire team each time one person leaves. The manager probably already has a list of skills the team needs so he/she reviews that list ensuring that the departing team member is not adding a skill gap to the team. If the departure does add a skill gap to the team, then the manager adds that skill to the desired team profile and prioritizes it with all the others. Then the manager begins to look for new skills to add to the team.

Key to Excellence#28: *Seek out diversity. Business background, philosophies, and intellects make the team better.*

The politically correct thing to say about diversity is that we should endorse it. We should have all sorts of diverse characters on our teams because it is good for us. We can learn more, understand differently, and become more open-minded to a large spectrum of ideas. Diversity opens up new horizons and new worlds for other team members and for our clients.

Unless you have actually lived with diverse cultures, business background, and personalities, you don't realize how true these statements are. One of the side benefits of working for global institutions is that you learn so much from other cultures. One of the biggest lessons I learned is that for an organization to be effective and profitable business does not have to be transacted the way that we do it in the United States. Other countries do different things because those things make it possible for them to be successful.

A little known secret about this global aspect to business is that a lot of what goes on elsewhere can be imported back to the United States. This then is the value that diversity has on a team. Diverse thoughts and ideas can differentiate your team so much that your audit process's value proposition is unique unto yourselves. Your "competitive" advantage is the results of your diverse thought processes and an ability to meld them into coherent audit practices. Don't be afraid of different thinkers; be afraid if your team does not think differently.

Talent wins games, but teamwork and intelligence wins championships.

—Michael Jordan

Key to Excellence #29: *Don't hire yourself!*

There is nothing more to add to this one.

It is All About Character

A key tenet of the internal audit profession is independence. Stakeholders expect the audit function to perform its duties separate and apart from management influence or dictate. This poses a significant challenge for most audit departments because they are paid by the organizations for which they provide work.

A number of organizations, if not all, make the appropriate effort to assure audit independence by have having the department report to the chief executive officer and to the chairman of the audit committee of the board of directors. However, not all organizations do the same and some auditors report to risk managers, chief financial officers, or even bank presidents.

There are also instances where audit department may include nonaudit functions like compliance, quality control, Sarbanes Oxley testing. One can argue the plus and minuses of these situations ad infinitum but that argument would be a waste of time.

The truth about independence is very simple. It is not about position in an org chart. It is also, not about to whom one reports. And it definitely is not about what else the audit department does besides performing audits. If it were, there would be no consulting audit activity. No, independence is not about any of that, it is all about character.

As an auditor, one who strives to be the best, you really need to capture this concept well. Some auditors try to be so independent that they end up isolated. Once they are isolated they cannot understand any of the nuances that occur in a business and impact the control environment. If you allow yourself to become isolated you gain no understanding of how management, both collectively and individually, manage their business. How people manage something is important to the successful auditor.

I have never struggled with this concept myself. I have embedded team members in a business and they have done just fine. I have seen some businesses only once a year and that too worked just fine. I have even done great business monitoring, some continuous auditing, and even served on special developmental project. All the while I remained independent. So how did I do that?

Actually it is much simpler that you might think. I define independence and "understanding my organizational role provides me an ability to express my opinion, based on facts derived from test work, devoid of management influence or personal bias."

In reality, that is all independence is. Would it not be foolish to believe that you could not work with your clients outside of an audit because it would impact your independence? When would we ever do consultative audit work? How do you build a working relationship if you are so independent as to never develop the relationship?

Let's look at the definition a little closer. You will note that the first part refers to the role I have in the organization. All I am saying here is that my role as auditor is not to run the business. It is not to make strategic decisions for the business. I don't make personnel decisions (although I can provide input into decisions that are going to be made by someone else) for the organization. Also, and this is a big differentiator, I do not _defend_ the organization.

Now some of you may perk up a bit here. You have read it correctly. I do not defend the organization. Defending implies a lack of independence. I am independent therefore I do not defend. I do however, "_protect_" the organization. Protecting the organization form failure through solid audit work not only adheres to the most valued of internal audit precepts but also confirms ones independence. By understanding my role within the organization I then can assure my independence.

The second part of the definition is the most telling for most businesses. If an auditor can express their opinion free from influence and personal bias, he/she is totally independent. This brings a great responsibility to an auditor and one, which in many cases, audit fails to uphold. Often there are situations where auditors feel that they cannot be completely honest because their job may be in jeopardy, or worse, their annual bonus. If you find yourself in this situation, simply get out of the situation.

The third part of the definition is the most difficult section of all. To be devoid of management influence is actually fairly easily. It is the last two words I want to spend some time on.

Personal bias is a hidden flaw that most auditors don't even acknowledge. Yet it does exist and it can have significant negative impact to one's credibility. Personal bias can be defined as a feeling towards or against a person, process, policy, or thought. While we all may have preferences, for example I prefer chocolate ice cream to vanilla, when that preference converts into a bias, it is harmful for us.

A good example of bias in auditing comes into play when discussing an organization's decision to centralize or decentralize operations. A study that was completed not too long ago confirmed that internal auditors issue 38 percent more comments or criticisms of organizations with decentralized processes verses those with centralized process. I know that you are probably saying that the results make sense. But do they?

A closer look at the comments themselves and the subsequent audit recommendations clearly indicate that the auditors in questions did not fully understand on simple tenant. It does not matter if an organization is centralized or decentralized. What matters is that management understands the different risk profiles of each strategic option and employs the correct controls to mitigate the respective risks.

Because the auditors in this survey made recommendations to "centralize processes because it would be easier to control," one can only conclude that these auditors did not know that ease of control is not necessarily the best aspect of control.

I have to admit, it is a lot easier to audit centralized controls. I don't have to think as much and the controls are pretty well obvious. I have to question, however, if my preference is objective. My own answer is that it is not objective at all. So while I did not abandon my personal preference, I determined to review only the risk profile of each different strategy. Thereby my own recommendations are addressed to risks and not to personal bias.

It is interesting because there is conflicting opinions about the same within management themselves. Having flexibility to respond to customers (decentralized) versus having a consistent customer experience (centralized processes) seems to be forever in debate. Perhaps that is why in organizational life cycles they appear to move from centralization to decentralization at least every three to five years. Sometimes even managers let their personal biases influence their decisions.

Key to Excellence #30: *Don't let personal bias influence your objectivity and impact your credibility.*

Another point to discuss when we examine character is the term "transparency." It is interesting to note that auditors in general are not very transparent. We tend to keep our audit plans secret, only sharing when asked. The business can never see a work paper. Seldom do auditors express an "opinion in waiting." Rather, they prefer to "wait" for their opinion to gestate before sharing it. Now the problem with this waiting is that once they express their opinion it is hard for them to move away from what was expressed. One would think that it makes a whole lot of sense to share an opinion as it is being developed so that erroneous conclusions can be mitigated. But who am I to buck audit history?

Auditors are very possessive of the information that they have in hand. Only recently have teams learned to share information and ideas early in the audit process with their clients. More and more teams are actually holding update meetings during engagements where potential issues are discussed and vetted. This is a great step forward; and a very positive one at that.

Even so there is something that the best auditors do that go beyond the sharing of potential issues. The best auditors have learned to share the "why are we concerned" about something very early in the audit process. This small step helps position the auditor to ensure that "why he or she may be concerned" is actually discussed in depth prior to anything becoming an issue. These discussions provide both management and the audit team an opportunity to pursue evidence that concerns are valid or not. Ultimately this transparency means that the audit process is more cost effective and less disruptive to your client.

When I have shared this concept with other auditors, I have gotten a lot of different looks and some ridicule. Many have said that we should not let management know of our concerns until they are fully vetted out. Others haves said, that we should not let anyone know the reasons we are concerned because then they will give us information or data that would change our mind and eliminate our concern. Others have even said that we don't have to tell management why we are concerned if it is a policy violation or process error, it should be obvious.

Well, certainly they are not the best auditors. Historical audit practice would probably align with those thoughts, at least to some degree. But if we look at each of them intellectually, they do not stand strong. In fact, I would say they do not stand at all. Let's examine each a bit more succinctly.

We should not let management know of our concerns until they are fully vetted out! Okay, so how do we fully vet out something if we don't obtain all the relevant information? Can you obtain all the relevant information without letting management know what concerns you may have at some point in time? Does it make sense to obtain

Daniel Clark

management's view on your concern early enough to determine if management actually understands your early position? If they don't, doesn't that tell you something in and of itself? The best auditors know that a complete conclusion on any potential issue cannot be arrived at without fully understanding management's philosophy and understanding of the issue as well. Waiting until after the report is drafted makes no sense to the best auditors.

We should not let anyone know the reasons we are concerned because then they will give us information or data that would change our mind and eliminate our concern. I apologize but I am unaware that auditors are restricted from changing their minds after additional information has been obtained. Further, I have not seen one audit pay plan that actually pays you for the number of issues that you report. It seems to make much more sense to examine every potential issue in sufficient detail to arrive at a conclusion. If information is found that changes and issue there is nothing wrong with that at all. This approach is usually reserved for clients that don't provide information throughout the audit. In those cases, the audit lead gets angry and frustrated and so places an arbitrary timeline on the business to provide information to the team. Failure to meet that deadline means that issues are in the report. Not a wise tack and certainly not a character builder.

We don't have to tell management why we are concerned because if it is a policy violation or process error, it should be obvious. Isn't this a winner? What auditor in their right mind still uses the "Gee, you didn't follow your policy as a legitimate justification for an issue?" Please don't get me wrong, there are instances where a policy violation is a violation. More often though auditors rely on this excuse because they have no other argument. What happens if the policy being validated is poorly-worded or flat-out wrong? Further, what if the violation to the poorly-worded policy was actually a good thing? Doesn't it make more sense to point out to management the weaknesses within their policy rather than say you violated your policy? Of course it does.

To summarize, the best auditors are transparent. They have a confidence in their own work and skills that allows for clear and unhampered conversation about potential issues. They understand that management, more often than not, will support a well-thought-out and evidenced position even if it is in the early stages of definition. There are times management will even help to get the right information confirming the issue.

So we have talked a bit about personal bias and transparency. What would a conversation about "character" be if we do not mention integrity and honesty? I will not spend a lot of time on these two items because auditors generally are honest and most have strong ethical values. I would caution you to be careful during issue conversations where negotiations take place. It is at this time when integrity may be compromised.

Key to Excellence #31: *Never lose or apologize for your integrity.*

Concluding this chapter, remember that independence is all about character and nothing else. Make sure that yours is never questioned by being transparent, always staying true to your integrity, and don't let personal bias or preferences cloud you objective decision making abilities. That is what the best auditors do.

Sending Difficult Messages—Yes You Can

Auditors are called upon to communicate different messages throughout their lives. One of the hardest messages to deliver is the difficult message. Whether it is to close an office, shut down a factory, to lay off staff, or to announce a failed merger, difficult messages are hard. Most people have not mastered an ability to communicate the difficult message. Chief Joseph did.

I am tired of fighting. Our chiefs are killed. The old men are all dead. It is the young men who say yes or no. He who led on the young men is dead. It is cold, and we have no blankets; the children are freezing to death. My people, some of them, have run away to the hills and have no blankets, no food. No one knows where they are—perhaps freezing to death. I want to have time to look for my children, and see how many of them I can find. Maybe I shall find them among the dead. Hear me, my chiefs! I am tired; my heart is sick and sad. From where the sun now stands, I will fight no more forever.

—Attributed to Chief Joseph, Nez Perce tribe 1877

In this now famous speech, Chief Joseph was delivering bad news under extremely difficult circumstances. Heading north to seek asylum in Canada, he had led a band of Nez Perce who fought the pursuing US Army for more than three months and more than one thousand miles. After a fierce five-day battle in freezing weather, most of the warriors were dead, and the rest of the people were facing starvation. Joseph decided the only option was to stop fighting and surrender to the army. The individuals he led were not obligated to comply with the chief's decision, but Joseph knew that almost all who heard his message would follow his example and surrender. In effect, Joseph had to advise them to forfeit their personal freedom, give up their ancestral land forever, and relegate themselves to living on reservations. Could there be a more difficult message to deliver?

Today, an auditor would probably never face the challenge of delivering a message as difficult and as far reaching as Joseph's. Even with layoffs and closures, people still have the opportunity to find other employment. Even moving to another state is not quite the same as moving from freedom to reservation living. However, many in business today are required to deliver negative messages to other executives, to boards of directors, and employees, and often find it difficult. Closer examination of Chief Joseph's spoken message holds lessons for those who must convey difficult-to-deliver messages.

As with all messages, and perhaps even more so with difficult one, the elements of the message and how the message is constructed are extremely important. What is the purpose of the message? What facts are available to support the message? What is the final conclusion?

Particularly important is the human element in the delivery of the difficult message. The person conveying the message needs to take into consideration how the message should be communicated, his or her credibility as the messenger, the likely way the message will be received, and the probable impact of the message on both individuals and the organizations as a whole.

Construction of the Message

Chief Joseph's message consists of an acknowledgment of the reality of the situation; the decision that has been made (which should be located early in the message); facts supporting the decision; and the conclusion of the message.

1. Acknowledgment of the reality of the situation: The tribe could not reach a place of asylum and would continue suffering if it did not surrender.

2. Decision: *"I am tired of fighting."*
3. Supporting facts: *"our chiefs are killed"; "it is cold, we have no blankets"; "my people, some of them, have run away to the hills, and they have no food, no blankets."*
4. Conclusion: *"From where the sun now stands, I will fight no more forever."*

Using the same structure for the content of difficult messages also works well today.

Recently, an audit team was asked to complete a postimplementation review for an organization that had purchased a new core system and implemented some of the basic elements too quickly. Implementation of some of the supporting functionality was delayed until a later undetermined date. Management told the audit team that the implementation had gone forward because the executive team wanted to "hit the market running."

At the end of the exam, the audit team delivered a difficult message to management:

"The company's implementation of the new Xwrite system was incomplete and mismanaged and resulted in a significant increase in customer complaints. Management failed to establish proper oversight, and no project management disciplines were put in place. Throughout the process, arbitrary decisions were made that increased implementation costs by 56 percent and increased system downtime by 78 percent. Finally, supporting technology required to be included prior to system "go live" was delayed. To date, there is no formal plan to implement these system enhancements and supports, which a full rollout of the system requires.

Note how the audit team used the same approach as Chief Joseph:

1. *Acknowledgment of the reality of the situation:* The business rushed to implement a new system to take advantage of the marketplace. Failure to include support functionality negated any marketplace advantage, as evidenced by system downtime and an increase in customer complaints.

2. *Decision:* Management must install supporting functionality immediately.
3. *Supporting facts:* Management did not establish a project management discipline for the system implementation, supporting functionality was arbitrarily omitted, early customer complaints were ignored, and no formal implementation plan for the supporting technology was established.
4. *Conclusion:* The implementation of the new system was a failure.

Note that Chief Joseph's message was clear, concise, and complete. It was also simple. No unrelated asides distracted from his delivery. No hidden messages detracted from his purpose. In addition, although he didn't soften the message, which could have been misleading, his humanity for the welfare of his people behind every word was in evidence throughout his speech.

The auditor in this example followed the same thought process as Chief Joseph. The message was clear, concise, and simple. There was no softening of the message, and the auditors concern for the organization and its customers was evident.

Key to Excellence#32: *Take time to construct the message properly!*

Human Aspect of the Message

Every message, whether positive or negative, whether written or oral, affects human beings. When delivering bad news, one must try to ensure that the message does not hit the recipients too hard. Doing so requires preparation.

Any messenger should consider three important attributes of this human aspect of message delivery prior to attempting communication.

1. *There is a rationale for the decision that is being communicated.* It is incumbent on the messenger to understand why the decisions conveyed in the message have been made. Chief

Joseph provided his reasons for deciding to surrender, which told his people that he completely understood the situation. The messenger should clearly explain the rationale behind the message—and there should be no anxiety about sharing the argument that led to the conclusions being delivered in the message. If there is anxiety, then perhaps the decision that precipitated the message, or even the theme of the message, is incorrect and should be reconsidered.

2. *Anticipate the likely effects on the recipient.* A sensitive messenger will understand the impact the message is likely to have on the individuals and groups receiving it. For example, when bank management announces a merger with another bank and says that redundant systems will require staff reductions, the messenger could also bring up retention bonuses, outplacement support, or severance packages. Providing practical and helpful information could reduce anxiety levels of the receiving the message.

3. *The purpose of the message determines its tone.* The messenger must decide on the tone of the message, which should be determined principally by the intention behind delivering it. For example, is the message supposed to inform the recipients or to elicit conversation? If it is to inform, the communication should be complete and not open-ended, as it would be if it were designed to solicit a response and evoke conversation. If the message is designed to elicit conversation, the discussion may even modify the final conclusion that is part of the content of the message.

Key to Excellence#33: *Ensure your message is filled with humanity!*

Once the message has been constructed and the messenger has confirmed the humanity of both the content of the message and the way the message is to be delivered, preparation must be made for the actual communication.

Preparing to Deliver the Message

Just as it takes time to construct a message, time is required to prepare for its delivery. Preparation includes rehearsing the words and delivery style. More importantly, it requires understanding the issues related to the content—the reasons for concern and the likely impact on the organization and people.

Understanding the content of the message—as well as the purpose of the message, as described above—helps ensure that the tone of the delivery will be appropriate. Many messages, both positive and negative, have failed to resonate with listeners when the tone in which they were delivered was inappropriate.

For example, when recommending a solution to a problem, the messenger should use words like, "you might consider" or "I would suggest." This way of couching the message indicates that the recipient has an option to comply with the recommendation or not. However, saying that management "must" take specific action indicates that there is no option. The tone of the message is much more serious than the tone of the recommendation, and it's clear to management that action is required. Confirmation that the right tone is being used can be obtained by having a practice run of the presentation with teammates the day before it must be delivered.

The tone of the message is more likely to be appropriate when the messenger thoroughly understands the content of the message he or she is delivering as well as its likely impact on organizations and individuals. Taking time to confirm facts and consider the messages' impact can also help the messenger be more poised and self-confident.

Key to Excellence#34: *Prepare to deliver your message by practicing beforehand and in front of people!*

Managing the Audience

Finally, no matter how well the message is constructed, or how much humanity is in evidence, delivering a difficult message also requires managing the audience. Applying the following advice will help increase the likelihood of the message being delivered well and understood correctly:

- *Research:* Prior to any meeting, research the organization, including its personnel and culture. If possible, find out the communication and personality styles of the meeting participants.
- *Organization:* An organized meeting is always the most productive. Prepare an agenda ahead of time. Time for free flow information should be allowed so that there can be adequate conversation to clarify the message for all listeners and allow them to discuss the potential effects of the decisions conveyed in the message.
- *Format:* The format and logistics of the delivery of the information must be planned ahead of time. Are presentation slides, for example, the correct format? Consider that slides have limited space so you will need to supplement them with oral explanations. Handouts, another option, can provide more detail than slides, but beware of being verbose and sharing too much. Bear in mind that people tend to read ahead so you may lose parts of the audience at different point of the presentation.
- *Time limit:* There is always a time limit for presentations. Actually, there are two: the scheduled amount of time and the amount of time the presenter actually holds the attention of the audience. You must plan for both, realizing that the most important time is the attention time.

Key to Excellence#35: *Remember to understand your audience before every meeting!*

Conclusion

Delivering certain messages may be hard, but it is part of what leaders do. The most successful will learn how to master the art and technique of developing and communicating facts, ideas, and decisions. Whether we aspire to be as noble as Chief Joseph or simply more effective at what we do, delivering difficult messages in the best way possible will certainly contribute to success.

Special thanks to Jeff Sacks who participated in this chapter.

You May Never Win the Pulitzer . . . But

The Secret to Successful Audit Reporting—Breaking Paradigms

Early in my audit career I learned how to write audit reports. This exercise, even after several "writing classes" seemed counter intuitive to me because much of my writing history was focused on creative, not business, writing. I found business writing a task where few people excelled. I also found most audit reports dull, self-serving, and, quite frankly, boring. The actual product of the audit engagement was, in the vast majority of cases, an extremely poor representative of the audit work just completed.

My initial concerns were confirmed by one of my mentors when she said: "The audit report represents your entire engagement. On the one hand, if written poorly, the readers will believe that the audit work completed was of poor quality as well. Even if you have perfect work papers or even elevate great issues, a poorly-written report can make all of that good work go to waste. On the other hand, a well-written report indicates that the quality of the entire engagement was top-notch. It can even make up for weaknesses exhibited in work papers or the audit process itself."

If what she said is true, then why do we spend so little time in training our audit staff to write well? Obviously there are classes or courses on writing. Consultants make a lot of money sharing the same ideas and styles, modified to eliminate plagiarism charges, but the same nonetheless. Honestly, in my humble opinion, most of them are junk. They teach an auditor how to complete a formulaic application approach to reporting. Typically, we see things like: *I looked at ten things, and four of those things didn't have a yellow letter. This is a problem.* Some classes teach you to copy your issue from the work paper into the audit report because you can then evidence or trace the issue throughout the entire process from discovery to reporting. Obviously, as professionals, we do not believe that anyone reviewing our work could do that trace themselves.

Much like Tolstoy or Dickens, the auditor must realize that the audit report is a creation. No longer is it appropriate or meaningful to just relate facts. There is no longer a need to maintain paradigms that are passé. The audit report is not supposed to tell the reader what you did, it is supposed to tell the reader where they need to focus resources, why they have to resolve certain issues, and provide an understanding why the auditor believes that the results of the engagement are relevant and meaningful. The report should provide "insight"!

So what holds us back? History; our bosses; the business? Sure, but really, it is just certain audit paradigms. Let's look at a few of these existing paradigms and break them right now.

Paradigm #1: Audit reports must reflect a rating.

A well-written report does not need the crutch of an audit rating to sell it. Consider a statement such as: *Controls over business continuity are poorly designed; therefore, the partial implementation of them is completely ineffective in mitigating the associated risks.* The reader of that previous sentence certainly gets the point. Do you really need a rating to say the same thing? As you explain the weakness in design and the reason why the controls could not be implemented in subsequent sentences, the reader will arrive at their own conclusion as to whether controls are satisfactory or not. However, if you are going to use ratings, then your report should reflect in tone and narrative, the rating assigned. My only message here is "Don't let the rating detract from the message."

Paradigm #2: Audit reports must show how much work the auditor did.

While it remains appropriate and desirable to include a section about the scope of the audit in the appendix of the report, why do auditors always use more words in this area than any other report section? Are we really so insecure in ourselves that we have to demonstrate in writing that we looked at twenty-seven processes, visited seventeen different locations, performed ninety-eight separate tests and arrived at this report that had no issues.

Scope statements should be short and topical. *Based on risk analysis of all processes associated with this entity, the audit team completed detailed control testing, performed several process walkthroughs, and reviewed significant amounts of business generated MIS to arrive at the conclusions in this report.* And if you want to go a bit further, and if it is appropriate: *The audit team relied on the results of the business self-assessment process, three external audit examination results, and its own business monitoring practices to support the engagement work. Details of all of these are documented in the planning memorandum which has already been delivered to management or within the engagement work papers.*

Paradigm # 3: Audit reports must include a management response.

This makes about as much sense as performing an audit survey at the end of the engagement. How many of you really believe that management is going to provide a sincere or accurate assessment of the audit in a management response documented in an audit report? If you have rated the audit, will the response not be reflective of the rating? I have never seen a manager respond to a positive audit with criticism of the audit team or process. And, to point, I have never seen a manager compliment an audit team when the audit rating is negative. So what is the purpose of management's response? There is none that would not been deemed political and therefore negatively impact audit's independence. Management should focus on answering the issues with well-thought-out action plans. There is no need for anything else.

Paradigm #4: The audit report must reflect the depth of the auditors work.

I wonder what the purpose of the work papers are if the report is supposed to do this? The report should represent the auditors reflections and analysis of the work performed. The conclusion of that reflection (or analysis) is found in the audit report and provides management with thoughtful conclusions as to the results of the work performed. Reports today present too much about the quantity of the work transacted rather than the quality of the analysis performed. In simple terms, we do not get paid to do test work; we get paid to provide meaningful insights based on all of the audit work performed.

The elimination of worn out paradigms will allow the auditor to actually message his/her report. By messaging we mean that the report has a purpose and theme. As such, the author only includes information that supports that purpose and theme. If the message is to tell everyone how much work the audit team did, so be it. However, if the message is to get management to resolve serious control issues, the amount of work and audit team does is somewhat irrelevant to that theme. Why then would we want to waste part of our reader's limited time distracting them from the real message: "You have these problems and need to fix them?"

Most of today's report writing skills are holdovers from the accounting base that audit's history provides. This base continues to be supported by accounting firms which, in all honesty, should remain detailed and general ledger driven. Unfortunately, internal audit is required to do much more than financial accounting auditing. To elevate our own performance and meet the increasingly demanding professionalism of internal auditing, there are many areas where we must improve performance. This auditor believes that we should not ignore the audit report in our analysis of better practices. The key to successful audit reporting is breaking the paradigms of the past.

The Secret to Successful Audit Reporting—the Power of the Audit Finding

One of the tools readily available to any auditor is the often misunderstood "finding." Whether you call it a finding, an exception, or anything else, there can be real power if understood and used correctly.

Most auditors use a finding to document an exception to process or policy. This then puts the business on record of acknowledging that there is something amiss in the area or item being reviewed. It also allows the auditor to document in their work papers that the exception was elevated to management and they agreed or disagreed with what was written.

As part of the overall issue processes within any audit methodology, this is not a bad step. Thinking through it though it seems to me to be one dimensional and ineffective when compared to a more holistic and risk-based approach.

A finding may in fact be an exception. However it may not be. I teach my staff that a finding is a "simple statement of fact." That fact represents the auditors understanding of that which was audited. This fact also is void of emotion or judgment. That makes it simple to write and simple to discuss. By presenting that understanding as a finding, the business can confirm that the facts the auditor knows are correct. Or management has an opportunity to clarify understanding and provide evidence that something else is what actually occurs. If in doubt, it helps to write it down.

I do not use a finding to confirm all my work because that would be redundant and provide no real value to either the audit or the client. However, if I am reviewing a questionable process, business line, product, or policy, then I always confirm any facts that may end up supporting my future issue. Let me give you a simple example.

One of my auditors was reviewing a process where overdraft for the checking accounts is provided by a credit card linked to the newly-opened checking account. The overdraft goes against the card automatically so that the customer does not have bounced checks. Then each month the customer can pay off the card. This coverage is optional and there is a nominal fee charged for the service which is charged to the credit card.

As the auditor walked through the process, there was some debate as to whether the customer received appropriate disclosure at the time of account opening. Someone said that it was verbal and done for every customer, while another auditor stated that the disclosure was sent to the customer after approval, which occurred several hours after the application submission. Here we had conflicted understanding so I asked my auditor to do more work and write the first finding something like this.

Finding: Customer Disclosure for Overdraft Protection

- *Applicants opt for the credit card overdraft protection at time of account opening.*
- *Applicants receive written disclosure related to the overdraft process upon credit card approval which typically occurs several days after account opening.*

These two facts, not at all threatening but completely accurate, helped clarify the situation and confirmed pieces of the process. Additional "findings" were then added color to the overall panorama of this process. In this instance for example, marketing may provide some additional disclosures that impact this product. Fees may be charged for this service. Also, the fact that the interest starts accruing when the overdraft hits the credit card is also an additional observation. Each of these facts may need to be documented as findings.

If the facts are accurate, the auditor can then aggregate the individual findings and provide the business with an issue highlighting that the disclosure process does not permit full transparency of consumer impact associated with overdraft protection. Then, the business can address the issue in totality rather than deal with a number of low-level or simple findings. This provides value to the business and helps protect the organization. Better the internal audit team finds and elevates this type of concern before the CFPB or other regulators do.

On the other hand, if the facts are incorrect, the business will provide evidence to that point and the potential issue goes away.

I would encourage every auditor to use the "finding" process to build your case, even if you don't know that you have a case. Findings help dispel potential concern as much as help to solidify real weaknesses.

The Cornerstone to Successful Audit Reporting—Constructing the Issue

There are a couple of very strong beliefs I have regarding our audit profession. One is that every exception is not a finding and the other, that every finding is not an issue. That may not align with your own position. In fact, some auditors are sure that they get paid by the number of reportable findings they have discovered. I have even noticed that our key regulators appear to reward examiners for the number of reportable findings they discover as well.

Having worked as a line manager for a large portion of my career, I fully understand the serious impact that addressing issues has on employee morale, customer service, and production. As auditors, I often find that we have little empathy for these impacts. Our only goal is to address the clear and present danger and we are really excellent at finding mistakes, errors, and process gaps. Unfortunately, that is not what audit standards expect us to do. There is not one standard that says our job is to find mistakes, errors, or process gaps. Why then are we so hell bent on inundating our clients with laundry lists of "findings" that they need to address?

There is a better way.

As mentioned in part two, it is important to write down findings. Once prioritized, those findings form the basis of potential issues. Taking time to review the findings in individual context as well as aggregate impact should lead the auditor to correct conclusion as to what is reportable and to what degree. Let's look at a few simple steps an auditor can take to construct great issues.

Step one: Review the exception for individual impact. Make a decision at this point if the impact of the exception, either on its own or linked to other findings, will be significant enough to report. If not, dispose of the finding as it will just clutter your thinking going forward.

Step two: Determine if the exception, now considered a "finding" is strong enough to stand alone or will be included with other findings in constructing an issue. If the latter is the case, combine these like findings together at this point.

Step three: For individual finding, determine if there is a significant impact to the business if the finding is not addressed. One rule I have is that if there is no significant impact then there is no finding. Auditors don't get paid to provide "Honey Do" lists to management. For those findings that do have a significant impact, determine what the root cause is and then construct the recommendation. A second rule I follow is that if the auditor cannot come up with a solid recommendation to address the concern, then there can be no concern. Auditors provide no value if all they do is highlight errors or gaps. Thinking through recommendations addressing issues indicates that the auditor knows something about the process and the impact to the organization that the issue left unaddressed would have on it. It also demonstrates that the auditor fully understands the impact of any solution has on the process. This translates into auditor credibility.

Step four: For aggregated findings, determine the root cause, the key drivers, align the findings to those drivers, and prioritize the findings within the issue. Aggregate issues should tell a complete story. Make sure to include positive and negative findings within the issue as this shows balance and understanding. By highlighting key drivers and then aligning your issues and recommendations to those drivers, the value of your issue is heightened.

Step five: Determine the issue and the impact. By focusing on the issue, not just the findings, you have constructed an argument that can be supported by findings and data. Ensuring that there is a significant impact because of these gaps provides justification for your reporting the issue. If you cannot come up with an issue or a significant impact, you have to ask yourself if you really have an issue. Don't be afraid to recognize that you do not have one.

Step six: Align your recommendations to the root cause, not just the findings. Too often we make a recommendation to address each individual contributing finding in hopes that the issue will be addressed. Don't do that. Address the issue in your recommendation. That way, the findings will be addressed (one way or another) but management is focused on addressing the issue, not the support of the issue. This is where the "cure the disease not just the symptoms" come in to play.

Following these six simple steps will help ensure that your issues are meaningful, valuable, and withstand the inevitable debate that occurs in every audit.

The Secret to Successful Audit Reporting—the Audit Report

I will not discuss the format of the report because each business is different and a certain format for one may be very effective while for another may not be. Rather I will focus on what really matters, and that is "the message."

A good report starts with planning the audit. I encourage my auditors to create the draft of the report (template) at the start of the audit. Then, as they go through the various stages of the audit process they can "drop in" ideas to that template. While most believe that this is a helpful productivity tool, it is actually a psychological tool because it keeps the lead auditor focused on his/her end product. In this way, the auditor does not get distracted by any number of minor concerns. Rather, they remind themselves that small concerns may become big concerns but only if related to each other. It really is not the quantity of audit findings but rather the quality of the finding that makes an audit successful. Even more important, the report must reflect those key issues correctly.

The structure of the report (not the format) should be just like a Tolstoy novel. There should be a plot (theme), some background to the story (entity history), character development (issues), and a conclusion. That being said, there is a big difference between Tolstoy and John Q.

Auditor. John Q does not need to write a 900-page audit report. So please, forget the prose and all the laudatory commentary. Be simple and concise.

A good example of this is when an auditor says that the business has robust or strong controls. No one has explained to me what "robust" or "strong" means. Isn't it more appropriate to determine whether the controls are effective or not? Why not just say "Controls in this area are effective"? Or the negative: "Controls are ineffective in this area."

I have to admit that I often laugh when I read an audit report that states that controls are robust, or strong. I know that my auditor is trying to give the business "credit" for having effective controls. Unfortunately, terms like robust or strong will not stand up in a court of law. Worse, the auditor looks foolish when one of the robust controls fails. Be careful and avoid using modifiers in your writing. If the control works say so, if it doesn't, just say that too.

Now, we are ready to write the audit novella. However, we do have one little twist! Our audit novella actually starts with the end first.

Telling the end of the story first puts a great deal of pressure on the author because now they have to ensure interest in the rest of the report. The best way to do that is to write the report in reverse. By that I mean start writing the report from the back page to the front. Start with the appendices of data and results. Summarize those and reconstitute them to the detailed issue discussion pages. Then move forward to the summarized and impactful version of those issues. When that is all done, write your executive summary (cover page).

Each of these steps is important because they represent something different for the recipients of the report. An executive may not have the time to read the entire report so the summary is a key for them. Middle management, however, may want to know a bit more detail so that they can support a thoughtful resolution to any issue. Finally, the auditee will want the details so that they can attack the root cause of the issue. In simple terms, the audit report serves many masters.

It is almost like writing three separate documents only these three documents merge into one report. Let's look at each section separately.

Executive Summary: Provides business executives a concise conclusion of the report and limited detail as to the key drivers of the rating. Also, executives like to know what the auditor thinks about the proposed resolution, so the summary must include the auditor's agreement or disagreement with management's response. A helpful hint in this regard is to consider the executive summary your written elevator speech. Two minutes to tell the executive what is most important. Be focused as you may not get a second chance.

After completing the executive summary, readers may want to know a bit more detail so they will turn to the issue detail section.

Issue Detail: Allows the report recipient to see exactly what the causes of the problem might be and what they need to do to address them. While this contains more detail, you still do not need to write a tome. The issue should be concise and clearly explain the concern and why it is a concern. The recommendation should be constructed to address the root cause of the issue and the business response will usually solve the problem. Please note: the business response does not have to match the recommendation. There are time when auditors forget that the best solutions come from those that work day in and day out with the process _not_ someone who drops in for a visit.

Finally, *Appendices:* These supporting addenda provide the reader of the report data, history, perspective, or other information that illuminates the issue cause, the impact, the prevalence of the gap or compares this information to industry best practices. These are often used to elaborate on the impact of the concern. These are particularly helpful to boards of directors or others who may not be engaged in the day to day of the business audited. Auditors often sell this section short because they consider it as a data dumping ground. The best auditors spend a lot of time on ensuring that the appendices provide value. Well-written and concise appendices can easily be the most vital part of any audit report. It pays to take time to write them well.

So what is the biggest thing to remember? While the audit report is the product of audit, it represents the results of the engagement work. It is not supposed to be listing of all the wonderful things that the audit team did. It is not a testimonial to audit greatness. It is supposed to tell management whether there are problems, what those problems are, what those problems mean, and why it is important to address them timely, and if management's actions will resolve the issue timely. That is all the report is supposed to do.

As a final note: it would behoove each of us to always write believing that what we write will end up in the hands of an attorney. With that frame of reference, the author will reduce reliance on emotion and focus on facts. Writing that the business has implemented very strong controls may not be the right terminology to refer to when those controls fail. Maybe, just maybe, it is best to write that "controls reviewed were designed appropriately, implemented properly, and should effectively mitigate known risks."

Writing a good report is not easy. But with plenty of practice and dedication, audit reports can become pillars of directive strength for any audit organization.

Connecting the Dots

An interesting tidbit regarding the audit profession is that we do a lot of work. It seems that most of us move from engagement to engagement throughout our entire career. There are even times when we are working two or three different engagements simultaneously. It is a shame that we don't have more time on each individual assignment because it would allow us to connect the dots.

Auditors in general are not very good at connecting the dots. The industry likes to pride itself on getting to the "root cause" of process errors or financial misstatements. But ask yourself, honestly please, how many times have you actually discovered the root cause of the problem? Now, wait: before you answer let me rephrase the question. When was the last time that you honestly found the root cause of the root problem when an exception was looked at in its totality and integrated state?

That's right. Finding the root cause of a single issue is simple. Because we are very good at that too many auditors close the books once they get to that stage. However, the best auditors understand that a simple one to one relationship is generally not the root case relationship. Why is that? Well let me ask you, have you ever looked at a tree?

A tree, if one were to examine it closely, as with most plants does not have one single root. There are many roots that sustain it. In fact, one root could probably be dead and the tree would still survive. It is the effective work of all the roots together that keep the tree growing and thriving. Auditors are good at killing individual roots but are not very good at healing all of the roots. I suggest that we need to eliminate the phrase "root cause" completely from our vocabulary. We all know what we think it means but that meaning is not complete. It is much more appropriate in today's environment to determine if all the dots have been connected.

Let me share a case study with you. You will note that there are several places throughout the study where everyday auditors actually stopped their test work. There was one, however, who went that extra step, connected the dots, and made a significant difference.

Background:
Red Fern Trust Company is a $6-billion-dollar trust department of a $35B Regional Community Bank. During the past five years, the organization has experienced limited personnel turnover and seen strong stability in the leadership ranks, including the senior vice president overseeing the trust department.

After several years of positive financial and audit results, including those from the external regulators, Red Fern has been beset by poor regulatory examination findings resulting in a loss of credibility with the exam team. Additionally, while assets have grown significantly, financial results are stagnant and have not grown as expected. Along with the flattening of revenues, the customer experience has been unimpressive and while customer loss has been minimal, there is little evidence of customer satisfaction.

The company has developed a strategic plan that will maintain organic growth plans and improve quality throughout the organization. It is hoped that by improving quality the customer experience will also improve. Enhanced quality will also regain regulator support and improve credibility of management.

Red Fern's corporate culture is similar to a small community bank. Emphasis is placed on satisfied customers (great customer service) and contented employees (fun place to work). These cultural goals have contributed to lackluster results and make it difficult to change processes, procedures, or improve the organization quickly.

The audit department for Red Fern has enhanced its own procedures and is engaging in the first risk-based audit of Red Fern Trust. These risk-based processes avail of data analytics that facilitates the audit process. This has been a struggle for the audit department as many auditors still want to perform the standard auditing that they have always done. The use of data analytics, while not foreign to the audit team, is something new because of the expanded use for this audit.

The audit team meets with the Red Fern management and begins the audit.

Let's follow an example of how one auditor, performing his/her assignment at a low-level process risk category was able to use and show how data analytics could provide significant value to the audit client. Building upon a singular test, expanding sample size to be 100 percent inclusive, and linking data from one test to another, the auditor provided his team with a palatable argument for changing the business model of Red Fern Trust.

So strong was the evidence and so well-constructed the recommendations, that Red Fern did indeed adopt the recommendations from this audit team. As a result, income has increased by 135 percent, employee morale has improved 25 percent, and the customer service experience has positively increased 78 percent.

(Authors note: while the audit was divided into several sections we will look at those that contributed to the aggregate solution only)

Audit Test Number 1

Objective:
Determine revenue generated by trust officer based on current performance. Consider dollar amount of fees collected versus dollar amount of fees discounted. Enhance analysis by adding the position factor into the analysis. Results are more equitable to the pool of officers reviewed. This can be aligned to revenue goals so the performance can be measured and appropriately rewarded.

Four factors considered in analysis:
Position of fee discount (officer compared to total as a percentile)
Amount of dollar discounted (total dollar amount in reverse order as percentage of total)
Position of fees registered (officer compared to total as a percentile)

Amount of fees collected (officer position to group in descending order)

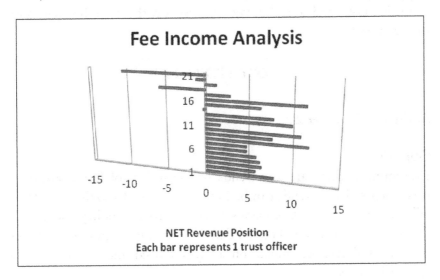

Findings:
- ❑ 3 of 21 trust officers exceed standard level 10
- ❑ 9 of 21 trust officers exceed standard level 5
- ❑ 4 of 21 make no positive fee contribution
- ❑ 2 trust officers discount fees to a degree that off sets 33% of the fee income stream from the entire team.

Detailed Findings:
- Total revenue via fees = $7.4mm
- Total discounts = $3.8mm
- Largest fee producer in time period = #8 @ $109m
- Largest fee discounter in time period = #21 @ $180m

Recommendations:
- ✓ Establish revenue goals for organization
- ✓ Measure fees collected and fees discounted
- ✓ Use analysis provided to monitor monthly and annual performance
- ✓ Incorporate into performance management process.

(Authors note: In the real case, the auditor completing the test actually stopped right here and wrote up the exceptions with recommendations. In reality, not a bad start, but you will see how there can be even more to this story.)

DON'T STOP HERE

Audit Test Number 2

Objective:
Determine if there are any trends in the waiver of fees charged to trust clients. These trends can be in the reason for fee waiver, the trust officer, the client, etc. Compare waiver to corporate policy and ensure that waivers met with policy standards. Note any exceptions. Consider the potential revenue impact on all fees waived and conclude as to appropriateness.

Audit Tests:
Review policy and procedures governing fee waivers.
Discuss fee waivers with senior management.
Requested a list of fees waived data by trust officer from financial reporting. Analyzed reasons for waived fees and categorized data by reason and by trust officer.
Added waived fees to discounted fees and included in income algorithm already determined to obtain enhanced numbers.
Calculated new spread on income/fees relationships.
Updated graphic.

Factors considered in analysis:
Dollar amount of fee waiver (officer compared to total as a percentile)
Rationale for fee waiver (determine if trends by TO, region, or office)

Results:
- Top performers remained top performers while top discounters also were top fee waverers.
- Fees waived accounted for $1.8m dollars of lost revenue.

- Business did not have a compensating factor for fee waivers as trust officers paid salary plus bonus.
- Bonus process did not consider fee waivers in calculation methodology.
- Performance evaluations did not include fee waiver management or performance indicators.

Detailed Findings:
- Total lost revenue via waiver = $1.8mm
- Largest fee producer in time period - #8 @ $109m
- Largest fee waverer in time period – #21 @ $180m

Recommendations:
- ✓ Enhance fee waiver policy to include performance management disciplines.
- ✓ Incorporate the dollar amount of fee waivers into performance management and incentive payout processes.
- ✓ Report lost income opportunity to trust committee.
- ✓ Analyze market practices regarding fee waivers and modify policy according to results.

(Authors note: Again anther test done with issue and recommendations. The auditor in this case also stopped her work at this point.)

DON'T STOP HERE

Audit Test Number 3

Objectives:
Determine if performance management process aligns to results. This includes incentive program payouts, salary increases, job alignment, and promotions. Specifically, determine the good performance is rewarded according to policy and problem performance is mitigated through development, coaching, or termination.

Audit Tests:

Review policy and procedures governing performance management and test compliance.

Review incentive plans, payouts, history, and approvals.

Sample performance evaluations of trust officers and link to promotions and/or incentive payouts.

Compare the performance evaluation ratings to income results.

Highlighted any commentary regarding income, discounts, or fee waivers.

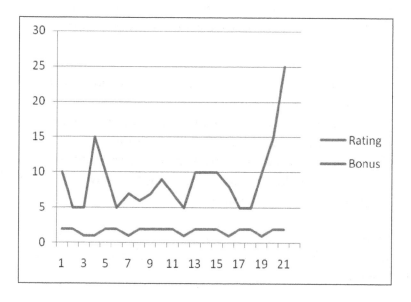

Results:

- No difference in ratings of top income producers or bottom producers.
- No performance evaluation included fees discounted, waived or income as a goal or a measured performance indicator.
- Bonus paid not directly linked to negative aspect of income, only positive income contributions. Negative aspects not included in bonus calculations.

Recommendations:

- Redesign bonus payout to include excess fee discounts and waivers as a negative contributor to bonus qualification.

- Enhance performance management to include fee management concepts.
- Amend policy to add fee management items with more clarity.

DON'T STOP HERE

Audit Test Number 4

Objectives:
Determine percentages of time spent by each trust officer in three categories: administration tasks, sales, and quality service which includes documentation, account reviews, other quality related aspects of the business.

Audit Steps:
Interviewed a sample of trust officers.
Determined amount of time spent on sales, customer service, administration, account quality (i.e., documentation, form completion, etc.).
Compared results of interviews with performance results.

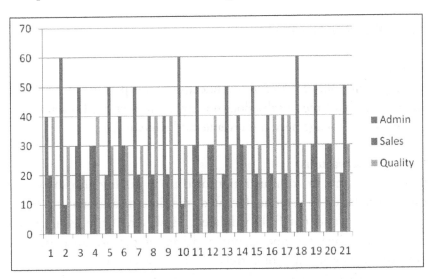

Results:

- Top performers spent more time on sales than on admin or quality.
- TOs spending more than 40 percent of time on quality.
- Less time spent on quality resulted in more waived fees and more discounted fees.
- Top income performers spent more "after hours" working on administration and quality items.
- All TOs felt hamstrung by amount of administration and quality work required.
- Thirty percent interviewed lost potential customers because of inability to get back to them in a reasonable time.
- Forty percent lost customers because of the amount of paperwork required.

Recommendations:

- Alleviate quality and administrative tasks from top producers.
- Train TOs on quality process to streamline requirements.
- Establish QC process earlier in workflow to free up time.

> **DON'T STOP HERE**

Audit Test Number 5

Highlights:

No apparent linkage between revenue and bonus payout.
Interesting that time in sales does not equate to increased revenues
No apparent linkage between revenue and time in sales

Other Observations:

Comparing time in administration or time in quality also shows not direct correlation to revenue. Granted, the time measurement is based on interviews and not fully validated. However, if the assumptions are correct, then revenue is not a driver of performance because performance ratings do not correlate to revenue either.

It appears that the business does not define performance criteria in a way that can be measured. Further they do not measure performance to key performance indicators that would strengthen the bottom line and support the corporate strategy.

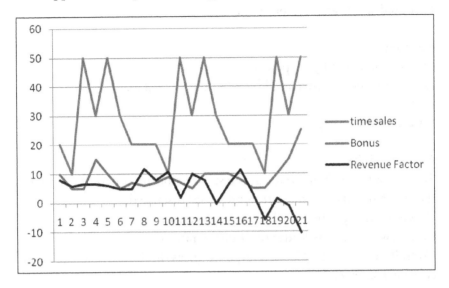

(Authors note: As you can see two more tests with good results and some good recommendation. As with the earlier examples, the auditor, whether due to time constraints, lack of experience, or any other reason, decided to stop the work paper on this test.)

DON'T STOP HERE

Audit Test Number 6

(Authors note: This test is a general observation test that was located in another part of the audit test program. As with all the others, each auditor did a good job on their individual assignments. This is normal protocol for most audit teams. Programs are divided into sections that one or more auditors can perform. Once the test is done, the next test is worked on. While this process contributes to the implied problem let us be honest enough to refute that that reason is the driver. Read on!)
Financial Results

Audit Activity:
Gather revenue numbers for past twelve months

Added back discounts and fees waived
Totaled revised income numbers
Projected five years income trend

Results:
Income increased by 35 percent year 1
Long term income increased by 125 percent years 2–5

Strategic Planning

Audit Activity:
The lead auditor then looked at the strategic business plan for trust and there was no change to existing processes discussed.
Received strategic plan and reviewed its detail
Interviewed business leader to discuss strategy
Overall strategy, BAU with organic growth: improve quality and customer service.

Results:
No deviation from plan of last three years.
Slow growth, more organic i.e., from customer referrals.
Improve quality, streamline process, and enhance customer experience.
Interview confirmed written plan—
Slow growth in income—
No deviation from current fee structure or processes.

Recommendations:
Develop MIS to track adherence to strategic plan.
Define terms within the plan.
Reconsider growth opportunities in light of analysis as internal growth can also meet the strategic goals of organic growth.

DON'T STOP HERE

Before we get to the conclusion let me point out that up to this point you have read individual audit test work papers that are stand alone in content and impact. I will not say that any one of these work papers is weak or that they should not be shared with someone. My comment here is that there are better conclusions and stronger, more impactful, recommendations to be made. In fact, the value proposition of the best auditor is greatly enhanced by taking one additional step.

Because you want to be the best you can be, let me share that step with you. It is quite simple to get there. All you have to do is connect the dots. Relook at all the work completed and see how they relate one to the other. Sometimes it will be obvious and others will require a little more understanding. When we connect the dots in this instance we arrive at the following conclusions.

Conclusions

Looking at all the information, the lead auditor decided to recommend changes to the current business model. By projecting potential revenues by trust officer he/she was able to show a significant increase in revenue, improved quality, and enhance the customer experience. Additionally, the changes would motivate trust officers thereby increasing revenues even more.

Some considerations:
- Could still use discounts and waive fees if total trust officer portfolio performance was positive
- Set goals for trust officers related to net income
- Limit fee waivers
- Limit discounts
- Incent for net income but include all income factors
- Trust officers that exceed standard 10 get to hire an assistance to support quality and nonsales activities
- Cost of assistant (fully loaded $82,300 annually)
- Increased revenues minus assistant costs (4 @ 82,300) $2.6mm

Recommendation given the business:
The business should revise their performance management policies and processes so that trust officers are rewarded for financial contribution to the organization and alignment with the strategic plan. As part of this revision management should consider, at a minimum:

✓ Restructuring the fee discount and fee waiver processes/policies in order to maximize account profitability.
✓ Directly linking incentive plans to revenue generated.
✓ Directly linking performance management to revenue generated. This would be in addition to current practices of linking quality and service factors in the performance evaluation process.
✓ Replacing poorly performing trust officers.
✓ Revisiting the business model and initiate the hiring of trust officer assistants for those trust officers that meet revenue standards (this allows the sales oriented TOs to excel at sales and drive revenue while the assistants ensure quality and administrative tasks occur as required).
✓ Enhancing MIS to measure and report on the revised performance standards.

Results:
• New ideas implemented, profits increase 135 percent within eight months.
• Fee waivers decreased 70percent and discounts reduced by 65 percent in the same time frame.
• Net growth in number of accounts 23 percent.

STOP HERE

Case Study—Connecting the Dots—Summary

1. Auditor looking to determine lost revenue opportunities. Reviewed "Revenue by Trust Officer" and compared to discounts by trust officer—results graphed.
2. Then ran "Waived Fee by Trust Officer" and compared the three.
3. Another auditor was looking at performance management and took the information from auditor 1 and compared to performance evaluations for the same trust officers and bonuses paid—results graph page 2.
4. Completed time analysis of trust officers.

5. The lead auditor took both auditors work and compared to business profits for the past twelve months. Results noted.

6. The lead auditor then looked at the strategic business plan for Red Fern and there was no change to existing processes discussed.

7. The lead auditor then did some projecting of potential income if organization structure changed slightly—top producers given an assistant to deal with quality—under the line officers let go.

8. New ideas implemented, profits increased 135 percent within eight months. Fee waivers decreased 70 percent and discounts reduced by 65 percent in the same time frame. Net growth in number of accounts 23 percent.

By taking a few extra hours the results of five different tests were combined to provide a meaningful set of recommendations linked to a tangible impact issue. The business understood the net result of the several issues and by structuring the recommendations together to point out the natural impact of the many causes, the audit team ended up with a valuable recommendation that helped management increase revenues by enhancing current processes. This is the power of connecting the dots.

So Who Are You?

So to move beyond the best requires a lot of work. It will not be for everyone. You should decide whether or not you want to excel. If you do decide to pursue excellence, remember this one simple fact: *Be who you are and make sure that you treat everyone else as valued treasures affording them the respect that they deserve.* Helping organizations succeed in establishing effective and efficient controls is all that we can do. We are not here to run companies, put people in embarrassing positions or have them lose their jobs. We are really here to simply ensure that management is aware of the risks associated with their business, takes them seriously, and designs and implements an appropriate level of controls so that their business will flourish. If we do that, we are the most successful auditor that we can possibly be.

So how do we get there? In addition to all the previous information, there is one vital step in our process: that is knowing who we are and understanding that truth in the right way. Let me share a story.

The Benefit of Saying Hello

The other night when I got home, my wife, Angie, told me of an interesting person she had met. Angie had gone to the gym, as is her daily practice. Usually the place is empty but today there was a young man, in his early twenties, already exercising. As is her custom, Angie said hello and began a conversation. Being of Latin heritage, Angie is warm and inviting and seldom passes up an opportunity to make someone feel at ease.

The young man asked Angie where she was from as he noticed her accent and realized that she was not a native English speaker. "Colombia," Angie proudly replied. Where upon the young man stated that he too spoke a little Spanish. Angie confessed that she was skeptical and that like most people, he probably knew a word or two (taco, hola, etc.). The young man then proceeded to speak Spanish as fluently as any native speaker. Angie was surprised.

As the conversation ensued, she asked this person what his line of work was. The man said it was hard to explain in English or Spanish. Angie, somewhat flippantly, said, "Well then tell me in Japanese or French," where upon the young man began to speak in fluent Japanese. Once realizing that Angie did not know Japanese, he switched to French, again fluently.

Angie was dumbfounded that someone so young had such mastery of so many languages. She commented that his language skills certainly put him at an advantage in the job market. He looked at her and very politely said, "The languages do not provide me any advantage. Instead, they eliminate a disadvantage."

Angie was so impressed with that perspective that she decided to use it with her clients (she is an executive coach). Not everything puts us at an advantage. Sometimes it just brings us to the same playing field as others or does not present a disadvantage. The subtlety of the statement is so powerful that it causes me pause as well. To know so much and feel that others are just as capable provides the humility that will powerfully drive his success. Western society places so much emphasis on "an advantage," that we often lose sight of humanity. This young man seemed to have understood that and did not let his accomplishments wrongly color reality. It appears that the more he accomplished the fewer disadvantages he had to address.

By the way: his profession? He is a philosopher of computer science. And to me, no matter what the language is that he uses to explain it, I have no clue as to what it means. But what I do know, the more I learn about my own profession, the fewer disadvantages I will need to overcome.

I tell this story because of the simplicity of a person's outlook. Obviously this individual was very educated and extremely capable. Much of his capability came from his uncluttered outlook regarding employment. He was not looking for an advantage but only to not be disadvantaged. No judgment made and no negative feeling to divert emotional attention. The most simple of words: "The languages do not provide me any advantage. Instead, they eliminate a disadvantage."

Whether this young man knew it or not, he actually shared with my wife his personal brand and it that point that is the last in our long journey to excellence.

BRANDING

Every person has a brand. Whether you created it for yourself through actions that others interpret or you painstakingly constructed it on your own. You are branded just like GE, Proctor and Gamble, Toyota, or any other brand out there. You have a brand within your family and at your workplace. When you interview for jobs, you are presenting your brand. Your brand, simply stated, is *you*!

There is value in developing and cultivating your brand. But you cannot begin to do that until you have decided on who you are and what you what to represent. I would encourage you to set aside an ample amount of time for this exercise of self-realization. You also will need to prepare emotionally and mentally if you want to experience success. Let me walk you through a process of self-realization that might work for you. This is not new age methodology or theory. It is actually a process that is based on sound business principles. After all, isn't branding a business?

Step 1: Gather all printed feedback from peers, employers, and others you have received over the past few years. Read through the information again, this time focusing on the aggregate message from comparing strengths and weaknesses. Write down those items that jump out at you that are consistent or noteworthy.

Step 2: Find and select someone to by your branding guide. This person is there to listen to what you discover about yourself, or how you are perceived, and to help guide you through the analysis of what it all means. This person should be totally honest with you and be able to provide alternative realities during your discussion. This is not a debate or a fight, so choose someone who will support the process not direct it.

Step 3: Gather more information by talking with a few select peers and coworkers. You may include neighbors or club members or church goers as well, totally up to you. In this step you are going to prepare specific questions to determine what your present brand looks like to people who are close to you or those with whom you interact in different scenarios. You can decide if your questions are only work related or not. That depends on the purpose of your brand and to what level you want the branding to have impact.

Step 4: Once all the information is gathered, create matrix and document the attributes of what people think about you. At this stage, don't be a miser and list out everything. If people say you have a great smile, write it down. If someone says you don't accept losing on the golf course well, write it down. Try and gather all insights into one location.

Step 5: Segment your attributes into common areas. Those areas might be something like work ethic, communication style, personality, communication, etc. Again you decide and let the attributes fall where they may.

Step 6: Set this aside and leave it alone for at least a week.

Step 7: Determine what you want your brand to be. This book provides several opportunities for reflection and even some directional notes if you are so inclined. Remember, your brand is you, so who is the "you" that you want people to know?

This step can be done completely on your own or with the help of others. You may already have a good idea of certain success habits and traits or attributes that you want to demonstrate. You may even have heroes that have inspired you and that you may want to emulate. Or you may have heard of certain behaviors that are success proven. Whatever the situation take plenty of time to create the branded you.

Step 8: Compare the attributes on Step 7 with the attributes in Step 5. This now provides you with a roadmap to your brand. The comparison will show you where you have already demonstrated, at least to some degree, certain success attributes. The exercise will also highlight attribute gaps that will need to be addressed if you are to achieve you excellence brand. You will also be able to note that some attributes which you possess may just not be as strongly evident as you would like. This provides you with the opportunity to improve those attributes and elevate them to levels more in line with your overall goals.

Step 9: Create a work plan to address the results of Step 8. List concrete action steps to help you obtain your desired end. These steps could be anything from education, gaining more experience, marketing the new you, or any number of things. Write down you goals with timeframes, milestones, and then share the final action plan with your mentor/advisor or someone close to you. By writing them down you are more committed to working towards the goals. By sharing them with someone else you are now committed publically to do so.

Step 10: Celebrate each achievement as a victory. This will encourage you to continue down the path of excellence branding and help you overcome the temporary setbacks that will occur.

Step11: Remember, branding is a living thing. Your base brand must be built on a firm foundation of ethics and morality. But there must be flexibility to grow and adapt your brand when necessary.

If you follow these steps, then over time, your brand will evolve to be the one that you truly want it to be and not one that someone else places on you.

So who are you?

The Final Two

The final two keys I want to share with you are the most difficult but also the most necessary. Chapter 1 talked a lot about insight. To be honest, while insight is important, there is something that will set the auditor apart from all others. That is the ability to share foresight with your clients.

No Longer Insight

I had an interesting conversation with a vendor (now a friend) just the other day. We were talking about the ongoing evolution in audit and she said something very thought provoking. For years I have carried the mantra that the value of audit is directly related to the amount of insight an auditor gains and shares. I define insight as knowing the intricacies of the businesses we audit; the nuances of the market place towards those intricacies, and showing an ability to analyze both thereby determining the combined impact to the control environment; and, ultimately, arriving at the nature of the business risk and impact of controls.

While my new found friend acknowledged the importance of insight she matter-of-factly said: "That having insight is not good enough. We should already be moving beyond that and demonstrate foresight in our auditing activities." She further stated that this is what executives want, what regulators expect, and what other stakeholders are demanding. Not one to sit around and wait, I have given this some thought, done some research, and have reached a conclusion.

My friend is right! Regardless of whether anyone expects it of us or not, internal audit needs to move beyond insight and right into demonstrating foresight.

Honestly, this will be a challenge. Many of our fellow audit groups are only now learning the art of insight. There is still so much to do within audit processes and education around this topic that many are not ready to even consider tackling the idea of foresight. But I have to keep moving forward, so to help us along let's start by defining both terms.

- *Insight: Apprehending the "nature" of things, especially through intuitive understanding.*
- *Foresight: Care or provision for the future. Knowledge or insight gained by or as by looking forward—a view of the future.*

Secondly, let's do exactly what Tevye did in the movie and play the *Fiddler on the Roof*. When faced with progress versus tradition moments, he measured impact and when right he moved forward with progress. So say good-bye to traditions that are no longer relevant.

It will not be easy this transition from insight to foresight. Just consider: *No one can predict the future! vs. People can be clairvoyant!* Or: *Those who fail to learn from the past are doomed to repeat it! vs. If we change one factor, the past will change!* Or even: *When hiring, past performance predicts future behavior! vs. People change so they will react differently!* And finally: *Past credit history indicates future credit behavior! vs. People learn from their mistakes!*

There are a lot of conflicting statements that have proven true or false depending on situational details. As auditors we should be able to sift through the conflict and arrive at thoughtful clarity. Can anyone predict the future? Yes, within certain parameters. Can you change the past? No, but you can interpret it differently. Do people really learn from their mistakes? Sometimes! It really is not easy to discern a correct response to any of these situations. Imagine how hard it then becomes for an auditor to gain foresight.

By removing ourselves from the inherent conflicts of future versus reality, let us hypothesize how auditors can gain this skill of the future, if it is possible at all. I call this the auditor's 5 Step Plan to Foresight

- ✓ Step 1: Gain or refine your ability to provide insight. By understanding the nature of things one begins to more fully comprehend the predicable aspects of behavior. Remember Success Tip number 1(?), if you don't have insight today create a work group that can help you obtain the knowledge you seek through their own experiences. This will cut your own learning time in half and you will be ready much sooner to move towards the future.
- ✓ Step 2: Understand the changing environment—there are indicators in the environment that provide a roadmap of possibilities and your insight will narrow those possibilities down into probabilities. Always remember that the environment includes your team, your company, your geography, your industry, and your planet. Global events do impact even small regional or community banks. Don't sell yourself short by forgetting about those items.
- ✓ Step 3: Use of data analytics is the key! Migrate to data driven auditing as fast you can. Teach yourself and your team the ins and outs of analysis, data interpretation, and data management.
- ✓ Step 4: Know what your business partner's strategic decisions are and on what they are based. This will provide you a general geography, if you will, of where you will be able to go in your discussions with them. Linking your foresight to their strategy will resound in a meaningful manner and they will objectively listen to your suggestions.
- ✓ Step 5: Finally, take a stand. Make a decision based on the information you have obtained. You can determine, with a good degree of predictability, what probably will occur tomorrow if some things do not happen today. Communication of your conviction will be the difficult part as many managers do not like to decide on things without concrete evidence that it has happened.

The future is now for the well positioned. Help yourself remain relevant by grabbing a hold of tomorrow today.

The last key to excellence is all about personal branding. You need to have one. This is not a difficult task because we already have a brand. However, I would encourage you to examine your present brand and see if it is what you really want it to be. The only question that you should ask yourself is: "Am I relevant?"

This is important because without relevance the ability to influence clients is based solely on the strength of argument. If a point is made solely on the basis of argument, then the influence that point has lasts for a short period of time. On the other hand, when an auditor is relevant, they are sought out for advice and given more opportunities to influence the organization.

So how does one become and remain relevant?

Assuring Your Personal Relevance

Let's start with a simple definition. Relevant means that we are "connected with the matter at hand." Now, anyone who has performed an audit engagement would be hard pressed to not be connected to the matter at hand. So on its surface this definition may imply that many of us are already relevant. That conclusion is a bit presumptuous.

Being "relevant" actual come from the Latin meaning to raise or lift up. This is the definition that each auditor should endorse and strive to meet. Presently there is a wonderful opportunity to fill an immense gap by living to this definition. Not only being present today, but raising or uplifting those you work with and those you audit.

I won't say that you will not have a good career if you do not agree with this approach. You probably will. But for those of you who want to go "beyond the best," this is the only way you can do it. In fact, the long term viability of you and your organization depends on your ability to prove your relevance. Any personal or organizational value proposition you may create is invalid unless it is relevant because of one simple fact: *Influencing abilities are directly linked to your level of relevance.*

Before we can hope to move forward and have work and a personal brand that raises or lifts up those we work with, we should destroy a few paradigms that continue to fester. Typically these are beliefs that are so institutionalized within ourselves that we simply ignore their impact. We may not even know that they are our beliefs. But for us to move forward, we must recognize them and get rid of them.

Paradigm—The more I say the more I demonstrate how relevant I am.

Auditors have a great desire to communicate. I have seen where this talent has helped paint them into corners, overkill a point to the level that no one cared about it or lasted so long that the point was totally lost. Aside from the physiological and emotional implications that accompany overbearing soliloquies, it really is bad taste to use an audit as a bully pulpit. This practice needs to stop because: *Relevance is exemplified by how concisely one communicates what clients require based on current focus.*

In my younger days I was lucky enough to participate in debate club. In debate club, you and a teammate are given a topic to discuss. There are always two teams. One team argues for the topic and one argues against the topic. The key is that you only have five minutes per side to express your point of view and hope to influence the judges enough to win the day. You are also given two minutes for rebuttal.

Not only was this challenging and fun but it taught me the value of short, concise, and influential verbal communication. As I got older, I realized that people much smarter than I already knew that and audience's attention time is limited therefore you needed to say a lot in a little time. With the advent of the technology age, attention spans are even shorter, or at least appear to be more susceptible to distraction. The best auditors understand this and have learned to communicate crisply and concisely.

Paradigm—The more I know the more relevant I become.

This is a hidden paradigm that is most evident by the auditor with six or seven certifications. Aside from the absolutely ludicrous ego trip this provides someone, an excess of certifications is one of the most costly and irrelevant things and auditor can do.

I know that this does not sit well with some in the industry. But honestly, they are not the best auditors either so it doesn't matter to me what they think. It should not matter to you either. If you want to be the best, you must focus you skills on that which you need to know.
I was the chief audit executive for a team of about thirty-five auditors in an organization that was well known for discipline and decorations, I mean, recognition. There was one auditor in particular that was somewhat of an enigma to me when I first arrived. He held six different audit certifications but he was just an auditor. He was not a senior auditor or a manager, just an auditor. Now don't get me wrong. There is nothing wrong with being an auditor. It is just that with so many certifications one would think an auditor would move up the corporate ladder a bit.

On the other hand, some people love to audit and don't want additional responsibility and this is all right too. Because I did not know what this auditors story was I decided to find out. I talked to the managers of my new team and to some clients. They were not impressed. This auditor, in spite of all the certifications that he had obtained, had absolutely no clue on how to audit. His work papers were unacceptable, he could not write well or effectively communicate with executive management. I asked why he was working for the team then. The answer was that he had a lot of certifications.

Please don't take this wrong. Industry certifications are a wonderful evidence of one's ability to study and master the requirements to achieve professional recognition. Most certifications are valid, appropriate, and welcome. I have three certifications myself. The problem isn't with the certification, it is with what the auditor does after they have one. In our conversation on relevance, the best auditors have mastered the art of translating the knowledge gained in obtaining the certification into strategies and practices which provide value to clients. A certification to relevance is like a policy manual to control. Policy manuals are not controls! It is the implementation of the policy that is the control. The policy manual is a reference and documentation of what should be. A certification may look good on a resume and even open a door but it does not make an auditor relevant. The ability to use that education appropriately will make you relevant.

Paradigm—I receive positive performance feedback therefore I must be relevant.

This is an interesting one. One would think that feedback would be a good measurement of relevance. In reality, feedback provides no confirmation of relevance. It only highlights potential areas of irrelevance.

That is a strong statement but hear this out. Most performance evaluations that are performed, and I have done thousands over my career so I too am guilty, are focused on technical aspects of performance. Did the job get completed on time? Was the staff developed during the engagement? Were the issues and report written well? There was never a question on whether or not the work was relevant.

In fact, if we use the Latin meaning of relevance I am hard pressed to find evidence that any work in my early career was uplifting, elevating, or relevant. The best auditors understand that performance evaluations do not determine relevance and so they use them for what they are, tools to improve performance.

Paradigm—I know I am right therefore I know I am relevant.

This is a fun one for me. I have known a lot of auditors and many of them fall into this trap. After weeks of testing, gathering data, and examining processes, the auditor has everything aligned and knows that they are correct in their conclusions. Sometimes they are and sometimes they are not. Whether they are correct or not is completely irrelevant. Being right does not make you relevant. Let me give you an example.

We were closing an audit in Chicago with a particularly difficult client. My lead auditor had worked in the business line of this client for many years but had been in audit for three years. We finished the audit and the lead began going over the issues. She came upon one issue and she explained to the senior executive: "Frank, I know this issue is correct no matter what your staff tells you because I used to work in the area and nothing has changed since I left."

Note: You know, my lead was actually right. The issue was sound and she had worked there and nothing regarding this issue had changed in three years.

Frank let it pass, which was a big surprise to me and the lead moved on to the next issue. After a few minutes, Frank motioned to me to see if we could talk outside of the conference room for a moment. Once removed from the rest of the group, he calmly asked me if my lead auditor had something against him. I assured him that she did not and he said, "Fine, I will take your word on it." We re-entered the exit meeting and closed the audit.

I still remember the event but do not remember the issue. I also realized at that moment, that in the eyes of this client, my lead auditor was not relevant. Nor would she ever be relevant as an auditor. She did go on to have a good career in auditing and then transferred back into the line, but she was never relevant to her clients. She had allowed her own emotions to override her ability to provide a relevant impact to a process weakness. Frank was a tough client but he appreciated relevance and he did understand the issue. His challenge was moving beyond the: "Frank, I know this issue is correct no matter what your staff tells you because I used to work in the area and nothing has changed since I left." I agreed with him then and I agree with him now.

In reality, being relevant is not a question of right or wrong. It is about being accurate at the appropriate time, with the correct information and detailed insight that can be understood, considered, and acted upon void of personal bias or prejudice.

Three Steps to Achieving Relevance

So how do we achieve relevance? Let me share something from Martin Luther King.

The first question which the priest and the Levite asked was: "If I stop to help this man, what will happen to me?" But . . . the good Samaritan reversed the question: "If I do not stop to help this man, what will happen to him?"

—Martin Luther King Jr.

I find this quote very powerful and extremely illuminating. The message of the parable was not that someone stopped (or didn't stop) to help an injured party, it was *why* the actions occurred. Granted this is a different interpretation that I heard in church when I was growing up. But as I read it I found that it completely resonated with me on all levels. Translating that simple story into auditing today, the very first step to being relevant is to invest in others success. It is not about "you." It is about your team, your client, your stakeholder. Invest in their success and you ensure your own relevance.

Secondly, the best relevant auditor audits to understand, not to criticize; they listen to hear, not to convict: and they analyze to provide value, not to support a case.

Another quote that I came upon is also quite illuminating. Tom Hayes said: "Claiming that you are what you are not will obscure the strengths you do have while destroying your credibility."

As I look back on my early career, I realize that there were several instances where I allowed people to believe that I was an expert in something that I wasn't. When it was discovered that I did not know as much as people thought I did my own credibility suffered and it took years of rebranding and hard work to overcome the negative impact. Relevant auditors understand what they can and cannot do. They are not afraid to let executives know that they cannot answer certain questions or that they cannot provide enough insight to shed light on a certain topic.

If you find yourself having trouble in this area, I would suggest you learn the following phrase that I picked up from the television series *JAG*. In one episode the judge advocate general was asking one of the attorneys for her opinion on something. The response, if I remember correctly was, "I'm sorry, General, I can't give you an informed opinion right now!"

What a great way to be accurate and ensure your own credibility. And this is the first secret of success in the path to relevance: Changing ones attitude from self to others for the right reasons will ensure you remain relevant.

The second secret of success in the search for relevance can be found in the following quote: "What man is a man who does not make the world better?"

This quote comes from the movie *The Kingdom of Heaven*. This is the movie about the crusades during the twelfth century and the battle between the crusaders from Europe and the Muslims of the Middle East in a battle for the Holy City of Jerusalem. If you take the quote out of context, one could believe that to make the world better meant that it should convert to Christianity.

However, the truth is much more subtle than that and evidence by a few minutes away from battle and the Holy City. The protagonist, Balian, inherits a lordship situated in the desert, several acres of dry desert with palm trees and a few cattle and other livestock. Balian notices that there is no water so he digs until he has a well. Shortly thereafter his land becomes rich and green. He had made this part of the world better.

An auditor can also turn the desert of auditing very green by making knowledge and experience their own. If you don't have knowledge, create a group to support you with experiences and abilities that you have not mastered. Then listen to them. If you seek expertise often, it will show that you are still willing to learn. In order to remain relevant, there has to be continuous education and learning. Only then can the best auditor make the world a better place.

One final thought in this area: *Give recognition to those who deserve it . . . and it is never you!*

The third and final step to relevance is found in the following quote:

Don't let your desire to be relevant stop you from being revolutionary.
—Mathew Barrett

I would go a bit further than Mathew in this regard. I am not sure that you can remain relevant if you are not a bit revolutionary. When I talk about revolutionary, it is not to go against audit standards or ethics. Revolutionary is simply looking at new and creative ways to perform your duties. Sometimes that means that you have to stand alone against many. Have the courage to do just that and it will help you be and remain relevant.

Let me give you a simple example.

When Everybody Else Does It—Should You?

There is a famous legal case presided over by Judge Learned Hand. Some call it the "That everyone else does it badly is no excuse case." It is actually the TJ Hooper Case of 1932 Tort Law.

For those not familiar with the case, TJ hoper was a landmark in tort law that established an important standard for negligence. The case was heard in 1932 to assign liability for a lost cargo. A tug towing the cargo on a barge had set to sea in good weather but later that night there was a storm and the barge sank. The owner of the cargo argued that if the tug had been equipped with a radio, the tug captain could have checked weather reports and taken the opportunity to seek shelter in a nearby breakwater before the storm hit. The owner of the tug disagreed and made a prevailing-practice defense. That is, that tugs at that time were not usually equipped with radios and this was considered normal practice in the industry.

In the landmark decision handed down by Judge Learned Hand, it was found that prevailing practice did not completely shield the tug owner against a claim of negligence. Basically the judge stated that "There are precautions so imperative that even their universal disregard will not excuse their omission."

Common prudence therefore was not always the same as reasonable prudence.

This was revolutionary at the time and as auditors we can relate to the initial premise. We often hear from our clients that everyone else does the same thing so it must be okay. The judge was right in his revolutionary decision. Today, auditors can be right in their revolutionary practices as well.

Keys to Excellence

#1: Build expertise through personal experience or the experience of others so that your intuitive abilities grow.

#2: Master the art of discernment. Things are usually exactly what they are not what people want you to believe they are!

#3: Be Flexible. There is always another perspective or approach. Be flexible enough to seek it out, understand it, and when applicable, use it!

#4: Never allow your integrity to come under question

#5: Always define terms and ensure full understanding before proceeding with your work.

#6: Remember to "commune" with your clients. Drive to common understanding and definition, not just of words and printed material, but implied realities as well. This means you may need to change your perspective and that is all right.

#7: Arguments are more easily won if the other person convinces themselves of the facts, issues, or the resolution.

#8: It is not enough to listen; one must learn what is being communicated.

#9: Study before you perform test work.

#10: Try something out before you audit (do-through) don't just perform a walkthrough.

#11: Seek knowledge from those who know through inquiry (your circle of counselors).

#12: Don't opine until you have enough information upon which to base an opinion.

#13: Don't judge intent of words, seek to understand them (ask follow-ups or confirm your understanding of what is meant).

#14: Clarification is not a sign of weakness. Make sure that you understand the context. In other words, know the reasons behind the answers.

 # 15: Hear what is not said and apply it to your learning.

#16: Don't be afraid to communicate what you really see. Debate is a healthy part of listening.

#17: Listen without prejudice. In other words, do not prejudge what you are about to hear. Listen to understand not to assess judgment.

#18: Don't do checklist auditing.

#19: Don't let the first answer be the right answer, unless it is.

#20: Ask others on the team for their opinions.

#21: Seek the advice of your circle of influence

#22: Don't be an auditor who cannot think.

#23: Don't overthink!

#24: Replace individual ego with team success.

#25: Relish your teammate's success.

 # 26: Always be positive in the face of adversity, especially in front of your team.

 # 27: Don't replace the person, replace the skills, or better yet, add new skills to the team.

 # 28: Seek out diversity. Different business backgrounds, philosophies, and intellects make the team better.

 # 29: Don't hire yourself!

#30: Don't let personal bias influence your objectivity and impact your credibility.

#31: Never lose or apologize for your integrity.

#32: Take time to construct the message properly!

#33: Ensure your message is filled with humanity!

#34: Prepare to deliver your message by practicing beforehand and in front of people!

#35 Remember to understand your audience before every meeting!